where
to go
when

DK EYEWITNESS

where
to go
when

Contributors Steph Dyson,
Taraneh Ghajar Jerven, Rebecca Hallett,
Stephen Keeling, Mike MacEacheran,
Shafik Meghji, Olivia Rawes, Daniel
Stables, Gavin Thomas, Aimee White

Senior Editor Alison McGill

Senior Designer Laura O'Brien

Project Editor Lucy Richards

Project Art Editor Ben Hinks

Factcheckers Edward Aves, Emma
Gibbs, Tim Hannigan, Georgia Stephens

Editors Danielle Watt, Rebecca Flynn,
Emma Grundy Haigh, Lucy Sara-Kelly

Proofreader Kathryn Glendenning

Indexer Hilary Bird

Additional Picture Research
Harriet Whitaker

Senior Cartographic Editor
Casper Morris

Jacket Designers Laura O'Brien,
Ben Hinks

Senior DTP Designer Jason Little

Senior Producer Stephanie McConnell

Managing Editor Hollie Teague

Art Director Maxine Pedliham

Publishing Director Georgina Dee

First edition 2007

Published in Great Britain by
Dorling Kindersley Limited,
DK, One Embassy Gardens,
8 Viaduct Gardens, London, SW11 7BW
The authorised representative in the EEA is Dorling
Kindersley Verlag GmbH. Arnulfstr. 124,
80636 Munich, Germany
Copyright © 2007, 2019 Dorling Kindersley Limited
A Penguin Random House Company

20 21 22 22 10 9 8 7 6

A CIP catalog record for this book
is available from the British Library.

ISBN: 978 0 2413 8559 3

Printed and bound in Malaysia.

www.dk.com

// CONTENTS

INTRODUCTION   6

// JANUARY   8

// FEBRUARY   28

// MARCH   50

// APRIL   70

// MAY   96

// JUNE   116

// JULY   138

// AUGUST   158

// SEPTEMBER   176

// OCTOBER   194

// NOVEMBER   214

// DECEMBER   232

INDEX   252

ACKNOWLEDGMENTS   256

Left Lush rainforest bordering a rocky beach and turquoise sea, Bali

Previous page An iconic yellow taxi in downtown New York City

Front cover Walking in gorgeous Alpine mountain scenery

// INTRODUCTION

Your bucket list is scrawled on the back of a well-thumbed postcard and pinned to the fridge door: see the Northern Lights dance across the Arctic Circle; celebrate the colour-caked festival of Holi in India; spot penguins posturing off the shores of Patagonia. But where do you go from here or – rather – when?

It's the most-asked travel question – "so when's the best time to go?" – and it's often this uncertainty that stops us from seizing the day and clicking "book" on that trip of a lifetime. Besides, we've all had disappointing travel experiences, when the timing just wasn't right. We were promised secluded beaches and instead found the coastline congested with sun-soakers. At other times we would have preferred the hubbub of human activity but the city streets were deserted. And don't get us started on the weather, when our dreams of endless sapphire skies were dashed by driving rain.

In *Where to Go When*, we've singled out the most unforgettable journeys, destinations and festivals for every month of the year, so you know exactly when to set off on your next adventure. Not only that but we've gathered mouth-watering photography that will stir your senses and transport you to faraway lands. We're certain you'll find new inspiration as you leaf through the pages. Perhaps you're looking for a getaway first thing in the new year, or you've earmarked September to October for a trip to distant shores. *Where to Go When* will provide you with a wealth of ideas – from electric events and festivals in Ethiopia and Albuquerque, through seductive scenery in the Maldives and Tuscany, to phenomenal wildlife encounters in Uganda and Borneo.

Travel adventures for every month, and in every corner of the earth, await between these pages. So pull up a chair, grab your bucket list and a pen, and let us show you where to go when.

Clockwise from top left
A reindeer in the depths of Lapland's winter; geisha chatting in Kyoto in early spring; the summer sun setting on St Govan's Chapel, Pembrokeshire; a flowering tree in Mozambique in August

// JANUARY

ST PETERSBURG, RUSSIA   **10**

LALIBELA, ETHIOPIA   **12**

JACKSON HOLE, USA   **14**

KILIMANJARO, TANZANIA   **16**

PATAGONIA   **18**

MALDIVES   **20**

TROMSØ, NORWAY   **22**

BANGKOK, THAILAND   **24**

JAMAICA   **25**

COSTA RICA   **26**

A verdant shoreline
along the island of
Dhigurah, the Maldives

Above The dazzling Church of the Saviour on Spilled Blood overlooking the Griboyedov Canal

Left Ascending the grand staircase of the Winter Palace; the snowy rooftops of the Smolny Cathedral and its convent

ST PETERSBURG

Europe Russia
ST PETERSBURG

WHY GO *January is in the thick of the Russian winter, when all those dreams of golden domes above snow-covered roofs, frozen rivers, hearty food and drink, and* troikas *(horse-drawn carriages) trotting along the icy streets come true.*

Not far beyond the borders with Finland and Estonia is St Petersburg, a Russian jewel that glitters beside the River Neva. Founded three centuries ago by the larger-than-life, modernizing Tsar Peter the Great, St Petersburg was conceived as, and remains today, Russia's "window on the west".

Peter created his new capital on a marshy site that had to be drained by the canals that now add so much to its beauty. St Petersburg's lovely, sweeping waterways draw comparisons with the likes of Venice and Amsterdam, and the splendour of its broad, planned avenues, monumental Rococo and Classical buildings and lovely parks certainly has a European orderliness and pomp – but all with an unmistakable Russian twist. The result is a visual grandeur that will take your breath away – most sharply around the stunning gold, mint green and white Winter Palace, over-looking the broad Neva, and along the main artery, the Nevsky Prospekt.

The Winter Palace is today the centrepiece of the State Hermitage Museum, home to one of the world's great art collections and the showcase institution of a city that has always been a cultural capital. Russian ballet was born in St Petersburg and its streets are still stalked by the ghosts of Tchaikovsky, Dostoevsky, Rimsky-Korsakov, Nijinsky and Pushkin, who all played out long passages of their often tragic lives here.

Spruced up for the 2018 FIFA World Cup, with dazzling creative spaces across the city, today St Petersburg has an excitingly dynamic entertainment and nightlife scene, plus a good variety of eating and shopping options, making it one of eastern Europe's chicest cities.

When Else to Go
May Several public holidays mean parades galore. **June** During the month of White Nights the city doesn't see the sun set, making for longer days to linger in the sunshine.

PLANNING YOUR TRIP Getting there St Petersburg has direct flights from many European capitals. **Getting around** St Petersburg's large, efficient metro is the best way to travel. There are also suburban trains, buses, trams, trolleybuses and *marshrutky* (minibuses). **Weather** The city is under a blanket of snow in January and temperatures drop further at night. **Average temperature** -10°C / 14°F.

LALIBELA

Africa Ethiopia
LALIBELA

WHY GO *Lalibela is affectionately called "Africa's Petra" thanks to its stunning rock-hewn churches. The town's unique mysticism is tangible in January when locals celebrate* Leddet *(Christmas) and* Timkat *(Epiphany).*

High in the wild and rugged Lasta Mountains, Lalibela ranks among the greatest religio-historical sites found on the African continent. The town's 11 medieval churches sit in carved rock recesses, their roofs at ground level, and give the impression that they have not changed for centuries; robed priests float among the dimly lit passages, and from hidden crypts and grottoes you can hear the sound of their chanting. The smell of incense pervades, while hermits, silent in the study of the scriptures, occupy tiny, rudely hewn holes. A steady trickle of pilgrims arrive, praying for health, wealth and good fortune.

This ancient holy site is at its most alive at the start of the year. On 7 January, the stream of pilgrims becomes a torrent as locals flock to celebrate *Leddet*, Ethiopian Christmas, among the awe-inspiring and truly unique churches. Then, on 19 January, it's *Timkat*, the day of Jesus's baptism. Processions, chanting, singing and dancing ring out from all corners and the town is coloured by the bright and beautiful textiles worn by participants. It feels as though you've travelled back in time. And in a way you have. Biblical it seems and biblical it is; as the second country in the world to adopt Christianity (in around AD 350), Ethiopia's connection with the religion is long and strong.

When Else to Go
October Fewer visitors, sunny skies and a lush landscape make for pleasant exploration.

PLANNING YOUR TRIP **Getting there**
International flights arrive into Addis Ababa, 640 km (400 miles) away, from where you can get a flight on to Lalibela. **Getting around** Internal flights are cheap if bought in Ethiopia. Car hire is available but expensive. **Weather** Lalibela's altitude keeps the heat down, with night temperatures dropping to single figures. **Average temperature** 19°C / 66°F.

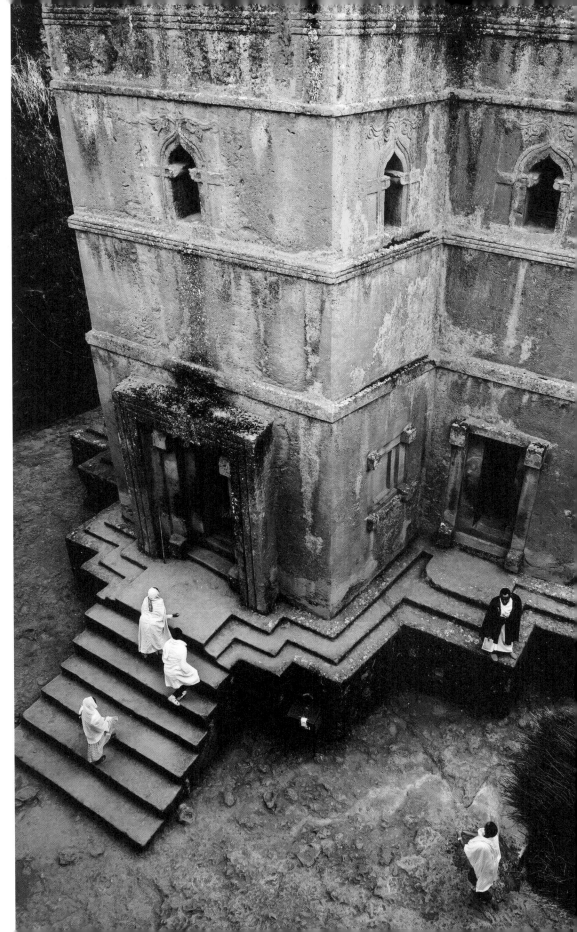

Clockwise from top
An Orthodox priest
entering a rock passageway
connecting the rock-hewn
churches of Beta Medhane
Alem and Beta Maryam;
devotees approaching the
door of Beta Giyorgis, or
the Church of St George;
a flock of pilgrims
surrounding the cross-
shaped Beta Giyorgis

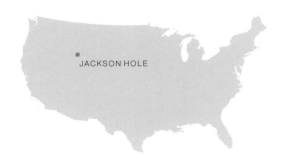

JACKSON HOLE

North America USA
JACKSON HOLE

WHY GO *Steep, deep powder and scenic beauty – this is the perfect time for all levels of skier and snowboarder to take to the slopes of Jackson Hole.*

Left and below Skiers enjoying the deep powder on the slopes of Jackson Hole Mountain Resort

Among skiers, the mammoth mountain resort of Jackson Hole is legendary for its challenging terrain, including Corbet's Couloir, a narrow plunge only for the foolhardy or Olympic contender. For the rest of us mere mortals, there are all manner of groomed pistes – called "trails" in the USA – for effortless cruising, and deep-powder snowfields that leave skiers and snowboarders desperate for more.

Situated in the heart of the dramatic Tetons, Jackson Hole Mountain Resort is in relative isolation in the northwestern corner of Wyoming. It is made up of two distinct mountains – Rendezvous and Apres Vous – which offer snow-seekers plentiful and varied opportunities. Skiers enjoy clear and sunny weather in January, with the average snowfall 1,200 cm (470 inches). One of the most ethereal moments occurs during a temperature inversion, when the valley is shrouded in fog but skiers above bask in blue skies; the sensation is of skiing off the mountain into the clouds.

When Else to Go
June Warmer weather makes for pleasant hiking around the mountains. **July–August** Classical music rings out across Jackson Hole as the Grand Teton Music Festival takes place across six weeks.

PLANNING YOUR TRIP Getting there The town of Jackson, Wyoming, has connecting flights from Chicago, Dallas, Salt Lake City and Denver. **Getting around** There are regular shuttle buses between the town and ski resort. **Weather** Can be unpredictable, with blue skies or monumental snowfall. **Average temperature** 0°C / 32°F.

CLIMBING KILIMANJARO

There are various routes to the summit of this iconic mountain; here are our top picks.

1 **The Marangu Route** takes five days and is the most direct route to the summit. It passes through cacti fields and alpine meadows.

2 **The Machame Route**, the most popular trail, generally takes six days. Walkers are rewarded with an incredible array of views.

3 **The Lemosho Route** still feels relatively untouched and is regarded as the most scenic. It takes around seven to eight days.

4 **The Rongai Route** takes six or so days. It has less traffic than other routes, meaning you have a greater chance of seeing wildlife.

5 **The Northern Circuit Route** is the longest and most exciting route. Taking around nine days to complete, the 360^0-views of the surrounding scenery are unrivalled.

TOP TIP

Remember that it takes time to acclimatize to the change in altitude when climbing. A longer route generally allows for more rest stops and a chance to acclimatize – plus you'll be rewarded with a greater variety of views.

KILIMANJARO

Africa Tanzania
KILIMANJARO

WHY GO *You'll avoid the long rains on the plains in January, making your ascent of kingly Kilimanjaro an even more memorable experience.*

The patchwork of savannahs dotted with giraffe, gazelle or zebra that you see from your plane signals a gentle start to your Tanzanian adventure. But don't get too comfy – you're about to climb the highest mountain in Africa.

As your trek up Kilimanjaro progresses, the landscape alters constantly. First comes lush tropical forest resounding with the peeps and whistles of bird song. Occasionally, through a gap in the trees, you glimpse a spectacular view of the plains below, a prelude of what's to come. Before long, the forest gives way to heathland. Giant groundsel and huge, spiny-looking lobelias colonize this corner, while birds and animals seem spookily absent. Then the heathland segues into desert, and altitude kicks in, declaring itself by

way of a thumping headache and seemingly unquenchable thirst. Soon tundra alters the environs again and you sense the end is in sight.

It's an early start at 1am on summit day. The tundra turns to dry, frozen scree, making the journey tough and treacherous. *"Poli, poli"* – "slowly, slowly" – comes the mantra of the guides, as a bitter wind blasts across the mountainside. At 4am, however, temperatures begin to rise and, like a stage curtain lifting to reveal a beautiful backdrop, Africa's plains appear. At last, standing astride one of the Seven Summits of the world in the silvery light of morning, it's easy to understand the lure of this great African mountain.

When Else to Go
June–October Visit to see Tanzania's Great Wildebeest Migration.

Sleeping under the milky way at Barranco Camp, on Kilimanjaro

PLANNING YOUR TRIP **Getting there** Tanzania, East Africa, is served by Dar es Salaam, Kilimanjaro and Zanzibar airports. **Getting around** Joining a tour is generally easier than tackling the climb yourself. **Weather** The altitude of the highlands tempers an otherwise tropical climate. **Average temperature** 28°C / 82°F.

PATAGONIA

South America
PATAGONIA

WHY GO *This seasonal journey takes you from Chile down to Argentina and reveals a landscape that is beautiful, desolate and absolutely unforgettable.*

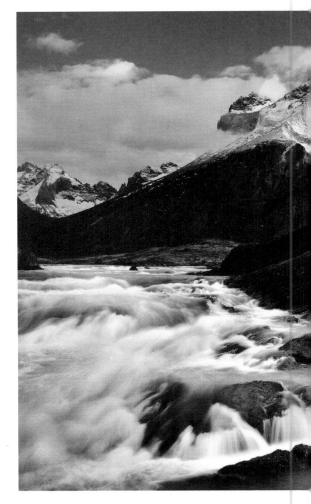

As dawn breaks on the Beagle Channel, the early morning light gradually illuminates the electric-blue ice of the floating glaciers surrounding your ship. The intense, wintry silence is broken by a thunderous crack as a huge chunk of ice detaches itself and falls into the ocean. This is southern Patagonia: a land of tremendous glaciers, dense native forest and incredible wildlife.

A cruise through the Strait of Magellan, from Punta Arenas in Chile to Ushuaia in Argentina, slowly reveals astonishing sights. Weaving through a sinuous network of channels and islands, the boat affords you a taste of this extreme land, from the vivid greens and fauna of the national parks to the biting winds that howl against the tidewater glaciers. Zodiac and walking excursions provide opportunities to explore this fascinating land and its outstanding wildlife. Around 4,000 Magellanic penguins crowd together on the Tucker Islets, their little black and white figures an irresistible spectacle. From the lookout at Pia Fjord you can see the Pia Glacier edging towards the sea, and, at the Tucker Islets, dolphins escort your ship into the bay. Looking out over Cape Horn and beyond, the sensation is one of remoteness.

When Else to Go
March Cruises are more affordable, and tourist numbers drop too.
November–December Warm weather and an abundance of wildlife.

PLANNING YOUR TRIP **Getting there** Cruises run from September to March. International flights land at Santiago, Chile; from here fly to Punta Arenas, the starting point of the cruise. **Getting around** Frequent port stops mean you can explore on foot. **Weather** Mild with some rain. **Average temperature** 14°C / 57°F.

PATAGONIA'S BEST NATIONAL PARKS

1 **Torres del Paine National Park** is in Chilean Patagonia and comprises mountains and lakes. The impressive Cordillera del Paine mountain range is the park's crowning glory.

2 **Tierra del Fuego National Park** is on the Argentine side of the island of Tierra del Fuego. The scenery here is vast, wild and home to a huge number of animals and birdlife.

3 **Laguna San Rafael National Park** is on the Pacific coast of Chile. The park is famous for the breathtaking North Patagonian Ice Field, which stretches across the landscape.

4 **Queulat National Park**, in Chilean Patagonia, has snow-capped peaks and lush forests. The park is home to the staggering Queulat Glacier, which hangs dramatically over a cliffside.

5 **Los Glaciares National Park** is in the Santa Cruz Province of Argentinian Patagonia. The incredible Perito Moreno Glacier (*below*) is found in this epic hinterland.

"This is southern Patagonia: a land of tremendous glaciers, dense native forest and incredible wildlife."

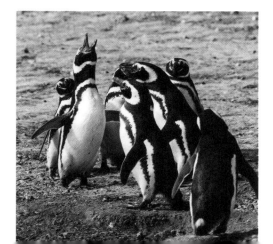

Clockwise from top Spectacular Salto Grande waterfall, Chile; penguins gathering in Patagonia; a ship sailing through Chile's icy waters

Idyllic sandy beaches and lush vegetation stretching along the island of Herathera, the Maldives

MALDIVES

Asia Indian Ocean
MALDIVES

WHY GO *The Maldives is famed for its exquisitely clear waters and sun-kissed beaches. In January, expect clear blue skies and little, if any, rain – ideal for unwinding in paradise.*

Surely the only way to describe this clutch of remote and tropical islands, each with its own coral reefs and shallow, turquoise lagoons, floating in the idyllic Indian Ocean, is "heaven on earth". Here you'll find coconut palms and fruit trees swaying in the breeze, and pristine white-sand beaches peppered with beautiful shells of all shapes and descriptions.

Time spent in the Maldives transports you far away from the stressful realities of modern life, and resorts are on hand to make you feel at home here in paradise, with a focus on rest and relaxation. Your body clock gets back into step with the simple rhythms of nature governed by the rising and setting of the sun; only primitive needs – eating and sleeping – exist and are easily appeased. The body is toned by surfing and swimming; the spirit is

revived by basking in sunshine and watching the spectacular sunsets; and the mind is rested. If you're feeling particularly adventurous, join a local scuba-diving expedition and discover the islands' magical underwater gardens, home to an astounding wealth of marine life.

It's warm and humid at this time of year, with a cool sea breeze breaking the languorous nature of the heat. The dry season runs from December to March, and though a gentle northeast monsoon hits the islands, the skies stay clear blue and the water remains peaceful and calm.

When Else to Go
March–April Underwater visibility is good in spring, making this a great time to swim with whale sharks and, if you're lucky, manta rays.

PLANNING YOUR TRIP **Getting there** Most international flights arrive at Velana International Airport, on Hulhulé. SriLankan Airlines is the busiest carrier, with frequent flights.
Getting around *Dhonis* (wooden boats) are a popular way of getting around, as are seaplanes. Malé and some larger islands offer taxis, but most islands are small enough to cover on foot.
Weather January has warm days cooled by sea breezes. **Average temperature** 29°C / 84°F.

TROMSØ

Europe Norway
TROMSØ

WHY GO *Time and place are both key when it comes to seeing the Northern Lights and January offers a great chance to cross the bewitching* aurora borealis *off your bucket list.*

Magical and mystical, the *aurora borealis* dances over Tromsø's inky night sky in a shimmering spectacle of exquisite colours. The intense green, red, pink and – on occasion – purple curtains of light are created from solar storms hurling charged particles into the earth's atmosphere but, to us, the *aurora borealis* evokes an extraordinary, ethereal illusion of infinity, a light show performed by the heavens. It's not surprising that the indigenous Sámi culture believe that the celestial aurora comprises lights shining from the souls of the dead, nor that the Vikings thought it was a bridge of fire built by the gods. Whatever the cause, you'll never forget the moment you witnessed the resplendent phenomena waltz against a cloak of stars.

Those searching for the *aurora* head far north to Tromsø, a city 350 km (217 miles) deep in the Arctic Circle, on the island of Tromsøya. Here in Tromsø and its surrounding wilderness of craggy, snowcapped peaks, the Northern Lights can be glimpsed from October to March, when the city sees 20 hours of daily darkness. In January, you have the best chance to enjoy cloudless skies, plus musical performances against the backdrop of the *aurora* as the city celebrates the Northern Lights Festival.

When Else to Go
February–March More clear skies to glimpse the Northern Lights.
May–July The ethereal midnight sun means endless days.

PLANNING YOUR TRIP **Getting there** Tromsø Airport is 5 km (3 miles) from the city centre and receives flights from Norway's main cities. **Getting around** City buses provide reliable transport. Car hire is a good option if venturing outside of Tromsø. **Weather** Snow is guaranteed, and wind chill makes the climate seem even colder. **Average temperature** -5°C / 23°F.

WINTER EXPERIENCES

Aurora chasers will find plenty to keep them busy in Tromsø and its surrounding Arctic landscape.

A wildlife fjord cruise is an amazing way to spot native animals, even in winter. Boats depart from Tromsø and passengers might see puffins, orcas and even humpback whales.

Fjellheisen cable car ascends Mount Storsteinen, which has superb views of Tromsø and is a great spot to see the Northern Lights.

Arctic reindeer encounters include sleighing and feeding these native creatures. Such activities highlight the lives of the Sámi people.

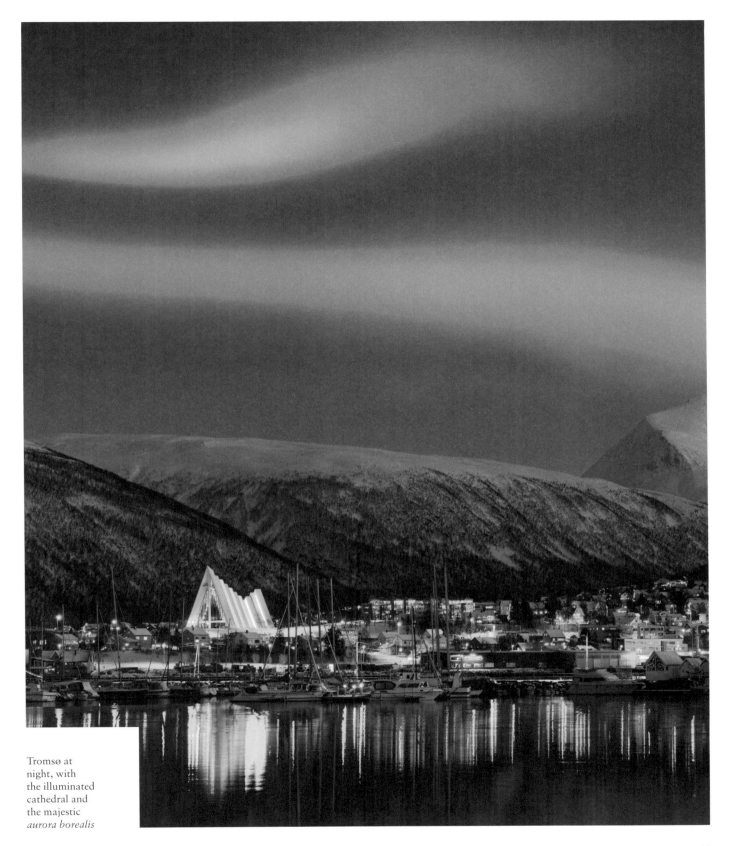

Tromsø at
night, with
the illuminated
cathedral and
the majestic
aurora borealis

Sun setting over
Wat Arun and
the Chao Phraya
River, Bangkok

Asia Thailand
BANGKOK

BANGKOK

WHY GO *January is relatively dry in Bangkok. Western and Chinese New Year both offer a sense of celebration.*

At first sight, Bangkok is an incomprehensible, sprawling megalopolis, home to more than eight million people and tuk-tuk tangled traffic. Look further and Bangkok has an astonishing beauty and grace: in the morning, watch the humid mist lift from the Chao Phraya River, revealing the golden spiralling towers of the Grand Palace and surrounding temples glistening in the distance. Stop and you'll see the small details that imbue life here. Shopkeepers present food and incense offerings to little Buddha statues; street cooks toil behind sizzling stoves; and monks carefully prepare the city's temples for the day ahead.

Founded in 1782, Bangkok was destined to be even more exuberant than the old capital it replaced, Ayutthaya. A sense of the past can be experienced in Thonburi, where the narrow canals wind through an atmospheric maze of stilt houses, temples and waterfront shops – a scene that hasn't changed for centuries. South of the city, the floating market at Damnoen Saduak is abuzz and its floating shops and restaurants are perfect for a wander.

When Else to Go
April *Songkran*, the Thai New Year, is celebrated with water fights. **November** Bangkok's Wat Saket is draped in red cloth for Golden Mount Temple Fair festivities.

Walking along
Negril's Long
Bay Beach at
sunset, Jamaica

PLANNING YOUR TRIP Getting there Suvarnabhumi International Airport is around 45 minutes by taxi from the downtown areas. Some budget airlines use the Don Muang Airport. **Getting around** The Skytrain is the fastest way to get around but it doesn't serve all areas, so combine it with boats, taxis or tuk-tuks (agree a price first). **Weather** Sunny and hot. **Average temperature** 32°C / 90°F.

JAMAICA

Caribbean
JAMAICA

WHY GO *Sultry and soulful, Jamaica is a heady mix of unique culture and cuisine, rich history, gorgeous beaches and dramatic scenery. The highlights of this Caribbean country are best sampled during January's perfect, balmy temperatures.*

White-hot beaches dissolving into bathtub-warm waters; sparkling waterfalls tumbling through emerald forests; tree-covered mountains soaring to 2,200 m (7,200 ft): Jamaica is a treasure trove of beautiful sights, but much more lies in wait on this idyllic Caribbean island. Clamber up Dunn's River Falls, sail down the Martha Brae River on a bamboo raft or seek out manatees in the swampy wetlands of the Black River Great Morass. Be sure to end the day at the Negril cliffs of West End, where you can catch a concert and watch the sun slide below a molten sky.

When Else to Go
July The sounds of Reggae Sumfest fill Montego Bay. Hotel rates are generally cheaper at this time of year, too.

PLANNING YOUR TRIP **Getting there** There are two international airports: Montego Bay (Sangster) and Kingston. **Getting around** Buses, taxis and hire cars are the best way to explore. **Weather** Largely clear and balmy. **Average temperature** 26°C / 79°F.

COSTA
RICA

Central America
COSTA RICA

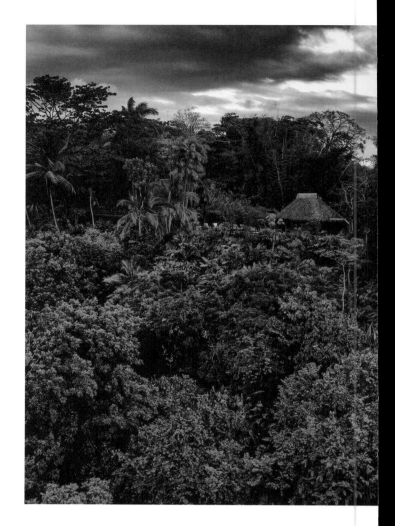

WHY GO *With a bounty of parks and wildlife reserves that buzz with wildlife at this time of year, Costa Rica is the perfect place to experience the diversity of the Central American tropics.*

Scarlet macaws screech overhead, howler monkeys swing in the dense forest canopy and crocodiles loll along riverbanks. This is Costa Rica, a menagerie unlike any other. The abundance of colourful wildlife is a major thrill of any visit to this tiny Central American country, where 6 per cent of the world's biodiversity makes its home. Cloaked in a thousand shades of green, the nation is a patchwork of national parks and wildlife reserves spanning 12 different ecosystems – all ready to be explored.

The mountain-top cloud forests of Monteverde, draped in ethereal mists, are a world apart from the tropical dry forest of the Pacific northwest, the mangroves of Terraba-Sierpe, or the lowland rainforests of Corcovado and Tortuguero – the latter a watery world laced with canals perfect for wildlife viewing. All along the coast, lush forests spill onto long swathes of sand where marine turtles deposit their precious eggs and paw prints betray the passing of a jaguar. Then there are the steaming volcanoes that stud the mountainous spine; dive into bubbling hot springs around passive Arenal, then peer into simmering craters from the summit of Poás. To the south the hulking grandeur of the non-volcanic Talamanca range soars and craggy Cerro Chirripó, Costa Rica's highest mountain, tempts hikers to ascend through cloud forest and *páramo* – a high plateau – for all-round views from the summit.

Stitching the varied ecosystems together into a seamless journey is easy given the country's small size and brilliant transport facilities. Many travellers prefer adrenaline-charged pick-your-own adventures as a way to immerse themselves in nature: quad-biking excursions, exhilarating zipline rides through the forest canopy, surfing in the ocean or whitewater rafting on the Pacuare or Reventazón rivers – with a wealth of yoga retreats and lazy beaches providing laidback alternatives. Whichever way you explore it, Costa Rica will inspire you.

When Else to Go
August–September Great whale-watching opportunities in the Southern Zone, as mothers nudge their infants to the surface near Bahía Ballena. **October** Límon Carnaval inspires a party on the Caribbean side, with floats, music and costumes aplenty.

PLANNING YOUR TRIP **Getting there** Costa Rica's capital, San José, has an international airport, as does the city of Liberia. **Getting around** All of the country can be reached by bus but it's best to explore by car. **Weather** January is in the dry season, and it's hottest in the lowlands. **Average temperature** 24°C / 75°F.

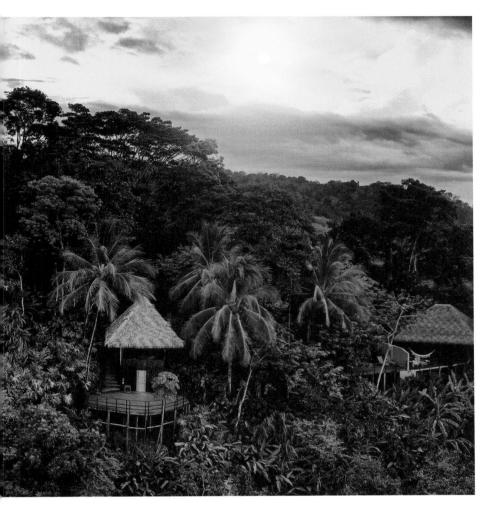

WHERE TO SEE COSTA RICA'S WILDLIFE

Costa Rica's diverse range of climates fosters an astonishing array of animals.

1 **Humpback whales** gather in the country's southwestern waters in late winter and late summer to perform spectacular courtship rituals, breaching the water and singing to potential mates.

2 **Brown-throated three-toed sloths** are found across the lush Caribbean lowlands. Look up from the trails near Cahuita and you'll spot moss-tinged adult sloths easing through the branches.

3 **Morpho butterflies** flash along forest paths in the gardens of Monteverde. The iridescent wings of these butterflies shimmer electric-blue when in flight.

4 **Scarlet macaws** gather in raucous, colourful flocks along the Península de Osa. In January take a zipline tour through the canopy in Parque Nacional Corcovado to spot breeding pairs.

5 **Olive ridley turtles** flood the Pacific coast in an event known as *arribada*, when thousands of females vie for space on the beach to nest. You'll see them on the shores of Guanacaste and Nicoya from July to December.

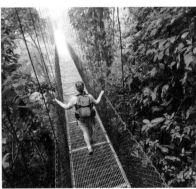

Clockwise from top
Corcovado National Park, Osa Peninsula; crossing a suspended bridge in Monteverde Cloud Forest; a red-eyed tree frog

// FEBRUARY

AGRA, INDIA   **30**

HAVANA, CUBA   **32**

OTTAWA, CANADA   **34**

ZERMATT, SWITZERLAND   **36**

ANGKOR WAT, CAMBODIA   **38**

MU KO ANG THONG
NATIONAL PARK, THAILAND   **40**

NORTH ISLAND, NEW ZEALAND   **42**

UGANDA   **44**

ANTARCTICA   **46**

MIAMI, USA   **48**

RIO DE JANEIRO, BRAZIL   **49**

Gentoo penguins
battling the wind and
snow in Antarctica

AGRA

Asia India
AGRA

WHY GO *February's warm, dry weather is perfect for enjoying Agra's majestic Mughal architecture, including the monument of all monuments – the Taj Mahal.*

As you wander around the preserved tombs, palaces and forts of Mughal India, you are transported back in time. The Mughals' best craftsmanship was reserved for funerary architecture and the Taj Mahal is, arguably, the ultimate example. As familiar as this incredible monument may be, nothing compares to experiencing it in real life. The marble absorbs and transforms in the light – a rosy pink in the dawn, white and pristine in the noon sun, dusky and sensuous in the shadows of evening, and ethereal and ghostly in the moon's diffused beams.

An hour's drive away is Fatehpur Sikri, the elegant red-sandstone capital that Emperor Akbar built in 1585. Walking from immaculate courtyard to courtyard, you can almost hear Sufi music coming from a nearby shrine, played for the dancers performing on the giant chessboard floor. Peer through the windows into the shady palace suites and picture them filled with the laughter of the harem as women float through the rooms draped in a kaleidoscope of fine silks and muslins.

Descendents of the craftsman who created these timeless monuments today sell beautiful marble inlay bric-a-brac and fine embroidery in the bazaars of Agra. This remains a city bustling with true Indian energy.

When Else to Go
October–November Cool, dry climate after the monsoon season.

PLANNING YOUR TRIP **Getting there** Indira Gandhi International Airport is less than 10 km (6 miles) from Agra. **Getting around** Choose from auto rickshaws, *tongas* (horse-drawn carriages), cycle rickshaws and taxis. **Weather** February days are pleasantly mild and the rains are yet to arrive. **Average temperature** 25°C / 77°F.

A boatman on the Yamuna River gliding past the Taj Mahal at dawn

HAVANA

Caribbean Cuba
HAVANA

WHY GO *February's sunny, dry days are great for exploring this historic city, while the cooler evenings are ideal for dancing the night away in a salsa club.*

Cuba's pulsating capital moves to an inescapable beat. Ever since the Tropicana exploded onto the scene, Havana's Afro-Latin music and dance have captivated the world's imagination. It all took off in 1939 when a brilliant idea was conceived in a suburban villa with a vast, sprawling tropical garden: rig an open-air stage through this jungle setting and fill the walkways with hundreds of performers, in thrall to a loud Afro-Latin beat, costumed lavishly and choreographed lasciviously enough to waft any audience away into an exotic wonderland. The Tropicana, which came to typify the pre-revolutionary decadence of Batista's Cuba, even survived the revolution. These days, February is the perfect time to visit. With very little rainfall – if any – you can spend a night in the balmy outdoors as the show continues on into the early hours.

Havana, too, like the Tropicana, is full of rhythmic sounds, and throbs with music: thumping Reggaeton beats blare from car stereos, waves rhythmically pound the Malecón and the sounds of salsa drift from the open windows of street-side bars. Poignancy pervades the city: patched-up dinosaurs of cars belch and clatter past crumbling mansions, barely lit by the street lamps. Start in the Old Town, Habana Vieja, and admire the grand Baroque buildings of Catedral de San Cristóbal and Palacio de los Capitanes Generales, whose rich marbles and undulating lines hint at a refined and wealthy past. Next, head to Centro Habana to admire the Capitolio, one of the icons of the city. Inside, take a walk through the sumptuous "Hall of the Lost Steps" and listen out for the eerie acoustics that give it its name. Later, visit Cuba's colonial past with a perfectly mixed mojito at the Hotel Inglaterra's rooftop bar and watch the stylish Cubans at play. Havana may be pushing on into the future – with a wealth of cool bars and stylish eateries now scattered across the city – but a haunting sense that Havana stopped in 1960 lingers on, making this one of the most fascinating cities on earth.

When Else to Go
July–August The Carnaval de la Habana is not to be missed. This week-long celebration fills Havana's streets with sound and colourful parades.

Right Vintage car on a typical street, Havana

Below The iconic dome of the Capitolio rising above the Gran Teatro; a barman making a traditional mojito

PLANNING YOUR TRIP **Getting there** The main airport is José Martí, located 15 km (9 miles) southwest of Havana. **Getting around** The cheapest and easiest ways around Havana are taxis, coco-taxis (motorbike-powered two-seaters), bike hire and on foot. **Weather** February is the driest, least humid month, with sunny days cooled by the northerly trade winds. **Average temperature** 22°C / 72°F.

Above Ottawa's Parliament Buildings overlooking Ottawa River in the snow

Left The colourful Tunnel of Lanterns, erected in Confederation Park for Winterlude; an ice carver working on a sculpture during Winterlude

OTTAWA

North America Canada
OTTAWA

WHY GO *Winterlude lasts for two to three weeks in February, but most concerts, races and activities take place on the weekends. Come for a short break to enjoy the festival and the city's highlights.*

Ottawa is blessed (or cursed) with some of the coldest winters of any national capital, which transform the city into a winter playground. The snow often starts to fall in November and hangs around until as late as April, meaning people have two choices: huddle indoors or make the best of it. Many Ottawans disregard the thermometer and spend the winter season enjoying all the sports, shopping and museums that the Canadian capital has to offer. Strap on a pair of ice-skates and join the locals gliding along the glassy ice surface of Ottawa's Rideau Canal, past elegant embassies and under arched bridges.

During Winterlude, Ottawa's parks resound with the buzz of chainsaws and the tap of chisels as artists create beautiful gleaming sculptures from ice and snow, and kids shriek on dogsled rides or have their flushed faces painted. When you eventually need to warm up, you'll find plenty of indoor activities across the city. Visit the antique steam locomotives at

the Canada Science and Technology Museum or the dinosaur skeletons and other fossils at the Canadian Museum of Nature. Don't miss the bustling ByWard Market neighbourhood, with its colourful street art, hip craft shops and eateries. The ByWard Market Building on George Street is home to a food market; stop here to feast on Canadian specialities including cheese and maple-flavoured chocolate.

As night falls, and the temperature drops even further, head to the warm, inviting lights of cafés and bars. On weekend nights during Winterlude you can join music-lovers wrapping their mittened hands around steaming cups of hot chocolate and huddling shoulder to shoulder to watch an eclectic array of bands. These outdoor concerts take place under a glittering canopy of city lights and twinkling stars.

When Else to Go
May Tiptoe through a million tulips blanketing Ottawa and revel in tulip mania at the Canadian Tulip Festival in mid-May.

PLANNING YOUR TRIP **Getting there** Ottawa is well served by international flights and the airport is 20 minutes from the city centre. There are also air, bus and train links from other Canadian cities. **Getting around** Ottawa is easily explored on foot. The O-Train and buses serve the city centre and outskirts. **Weather** In February the skies are generally cloudy; snow and/or rain is likely. **Average temperature** -9°C / 16°F.

ZERMATT

Europe Switzerland
ZERMATT

WHY GO *The powder slopes around Zermatt are at their best in February – your snow-filled adventure awaits.*

In this quintessential Swiss village, picturesque chalets dot the hillsides and horse-drawn sleighs ply the main street, all under the watchful gaze of Switzerland's mighty Matterhorn mountain. The friendly atmosphere during the day turns positively festive after dark, as groups of friends wander towards a restaurant or club, stopping along the way to window shop at the elegant boutiques along the way.

When it's time to hit the slopes you're spoilt for choice. Nearly half of Europe's peaks reaching over 4,000 m (13,125 ft) surround Zermatt and each summit promises staggering vistas. Choosing a gentle, groomed piste is a great way to let your equipment think for itself so that you can admire the surroundings. If you are an enthusiast, why not participate in the incredible ski safari? It's made up of three connected peaks: the Rothorn, the Gornegrat and Klein Matterhorn.

When Else to Go
July–August Enjoy culinary, music and arts festivals, plus superb hiking opportunities.

PLANNING YOUR TRIP **Getting there** Zermatt is accessible by train from Switzerland's Zürich, Geneva and Basel airports. **Getting around** The village is walkable (and car-free). **Weather** Sunny and snowy days. The mountain summits are very exposed. **Average temperature** -3°C / 27°F.

Climbing up to the starting point of the Marinelli Couloir, in the Swiss Alps

ANGKOR WAT

Asia Cambodia
ANGKOR WAT

WHY GO *February skies are brilliant blue and cloudless. Walking or cycling on the dry, shady forest paths around the temples is a delight.*

At dawn, as if on cue, the silence at Angkor Wat is suddenly broken by the piercing trill of cicadas. The first rays of the sun appear behind the darkened silhouette of the temple, slowly rising over the five lotus-bud-shaped towers and illuminating the long causeway. It is a magical moment in a mystical place that has witnessed each new day since the 12th century.

Aligned with the sun and the moon, Angkor Wat, with its towers, galleries, courtyards and moat, is the biggest religious monument in the world. It is alive with vivid sculptures and the morning light is perfect for looking at bas-reliefs of mythical battles that look more like ballets and scenes from Hindu epics. As you climb towards the central sanctuary, marvel at the detail of the many exquisitely carved *apsaras*, the celestial dancers, with their voluptuous figures, towering head-dresses and enigmatic smiles.

After such grandeur, head for smaller temples, like Ta Prohm. When you get to the temple, still covered in jungle, its collapsing galleries swathed in huge silk-cotton trees which prise apart the stones, it's like finding a lost city. Deeper in the forest lies an even older temple, Banteay Srei, a miniature, fairy-tale temple in red sandstone, covered with 10th-century carvings. At sunset, climb Phnom Bakheng, the temple mountain where, in the distance, you can see the five towers of Angkor Wat turn to gold in the fading light. If you are lucky you'll witness the flight of the bats as they emerge from the nooks and crannies to feed, before everything slowly disappears into the shadows and darkness descends again.

When Else to Go
October The end of the rainy season is a quieter time to visit, but be prepared for torrential rain in the afternoons.

Above Sunrise over Angkor Wat, Cambodia

Right Carved figures outside the South Gate; the beautiful ruins of Ta Prohm temple, with a tree lodged in the masonry; a Buddhist monk

PLANNING YOUR TRIP Getting there Flights arrive at Siem Reap, 6 km (4 miles) from Angkor Wat. **Getting around** Hire a tuk-tuk with a guide who will take you around the temples for a fee, or hire a bicycle so you can see the sites at your own pace. **Weather** Dry, bright, tropical and hot. **Average temperature** 27°C / 81°F.

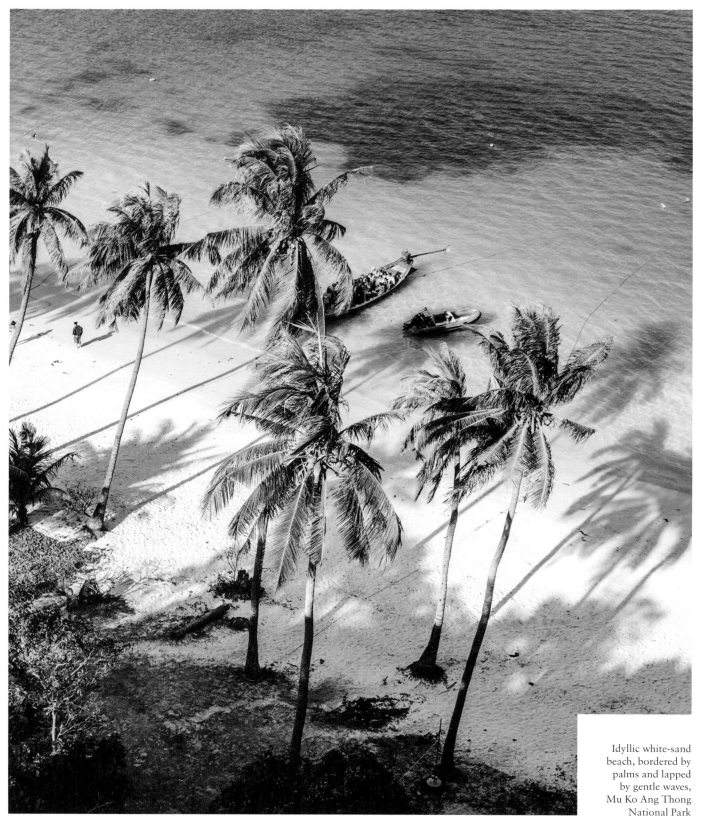

Idyllic white-sand beach, bordered by palms and lapped by gentle waves, Mu Ko Ang Thong National Park

Asia Thailand

MU KO ANG THONG NATIONAL PARK

WHY GO *You'll be treated to warm weather and calm seas in February, so whether you plan to snorkel or relax on a beach, your visit to this gorgeous national park will be unforgettable.*

The first approach to the 42 islands of Mu Ko Ang Thong National Park is always stunning. Rocky outcrops, covered with deep green vegetation, interspersed with hidden coves and sublime sandy beaches, appear one by one from the glistening turquoise sea. Their strange shapes have inspired appropriately bizarre names such as Neck Island, Sleeping Cow and Rhinoceros Island, which add to their mystical attractions.

The waters around the islands of Hin Nippon and Ko Wao offer some of the park's best snorkelling – the huge, brain-like corals found here are truly spectacular. Ko Wua Talab is a coconut-covered island with probably the most beautiful beach in the park.

But the true highlight of any tour is a visit to gorgeous Ko Mae Ko, where a mountain hike will lead you to a look-out over Thale Noi, a hidden turquoise saltwater lake. From here, you can see across the whole archipelago, as well as the two larger neighbouring islands that sit outside the marine park, Ko Tao and Ko Pha Ngan. Explore the clear waters around Ko Tao, which boast some of the best marine life that Thailand has to offer. Or seek out one of the many island beaches where, protected by limestone cliffs, you'll find your own secluded hideaway.

When Else to Go
March–May This is the best time to spot huge whale sharks off Ko Tao.

PLANNING YOUR TRIP **Getting there** Flights arrive into Bangkok, from where you can catch a domestic flight to Ko Samui. **Getting around** To reach the marine park, take a boat tour or hire a local fishing boat. Ko Tao and Ko Pha Ngan can be reached by ferry. **Weather** Days are warm and dry. **Average temperature** 27°C/ 81°F.

SPECTACULAR DIVING SPOTS

The clear waters and rich marine life in Mu Ko Ang Thong National Park offer superb opportunities for snorkelling and scuba diving. Discover coral reefs teeming with small fish and explore wonderful shallow caves. Here are some great places to get beneath the waves.

1 The beautiful corals at **Ko Wao** are home to angelfish and blue-spotted stingrays.

2 Vibrant sea fans and bushy corals make **Hin Yippon** a great spot for underwater photography.

3 See dainty clown fish and huge barrel sponges in the caves at **Ko Yippon Lek**.

4 **Sail Rock** is the most reputed dive site in the Gulf of Thailand. Whale shark spottings are most likely in April.

5 The waters around the tiny island of **Ko Sam Sao** have some of the park's best coral reefs.

NORTH ISLAND

Oceania New Zealand
NORTH ISLAND

WHY GO *February falls in New Zealand's summer, when you're likely to have the most reliable weather – perfect for exploring the spectacular North Island.*

Imagine a land where everyone lives within easy reach of lush forest trails, unspoiled beaches, gently rolling farmland and sparkling rivers. Where mountains are shrouded in legend and the surrounding islands are subtropical idylls. New Zealand's North Island has all of this, coupled with a sunny summer climate that is hard to resist. Hiring a car or a campervan to tour the island will enable you to really experience all that is on offer.

At its volcanic heart, vast lakes are cradled in ancient craters and towering volcano cones are powerful reminders of the landscape's turbulent past. In this geothermal paradise, the land itself seems alive; geysers spout plumes of boiling, mineral-rich water, steam drifts eerily across a lunar landscape and slurping cauldrons of bubbling mud plop lazily. These natural phenomena are key to the ancient Māori culture that can still be observed on the island. There's a real sense of openness here, in the landscape and the friendliness of its people. The North Island will astound you and fill your mind with countless picture-postcard scenes.

When Else to Go
September Wellington, New Zealand's capital city, hosts its famous two-week World of WearableArt festival, featuring spectactular garments. Book tickets and accommodation well in advance.

PLANNING YOUR TRIP **Getting there** Most international flights arrive in Auckland. **Getting around** Car and campervan hire is available in cities, major towns and airports. **Weather** February is warm but changeable. **Average temperature** 24–30°C / 75–86°F.

Right Steam drifting across Champagne Pool at Wai-O-Tapu Thermal Wonderland near Rotorua, North Island

Below Fern leaves, a common sight in New Zealand; a Māori whakairo rākau (wood carving)

UGANDA

Africa
UGANDA

WHY GO *As the forest canopy thins out during Uganda's dry season, spotting gorillas on a trek becomes an exciting possibility.*

The atmosphere in the distinctly thick jungle of Bwindi Impenetrable National Park, located in one of earth's wildest regions, is so tense and charged you can almost hear it crackle. This uncultivated rainforest is the habitat of some of Africa's last troops of mountain gorillas. It's as difficult to navigate as the park's name suggests, and finding a path through the thick and thorny primeval wood – on a fantasy expedition to find the elusive apes – is as off-script as it is unexpected. Shadows play tricks on you from under every branch as you climb steep verges and cross rivers.

The jungle, a rough-and-tumble, day-long drive west of Entebbe or Kampala, is a place of rainforest canopies, Tarzan vines and buffers of rugged vegetation. While gorillas are the main draw, that's only the beginning. Keep an eye out for red-tailed monkeys, chimpanzees, jungle-residing elephants and giant forest hogs.

The truth is you just have to get out there. Only then will you hear the wind whispering through all those leaves and realise there's a silverback before you.

When Else to Go
September–November Although the weather is generally misty and wet, this is the best time for bird-watching in the forest.

PLANNING YOUR TRIP **Getting there** Fly from Entebbe, Uganda's main airport, to the Kisoro airstrip, or drive from Entebbe or Kampala. **Getting around** The Bwindi park is best accessed as part of an overland tour or multi-day safari. Purchase gorilla trekking permits in advance. **Weather** Dry and hot. **Average temperature** 24°C / 75°F.

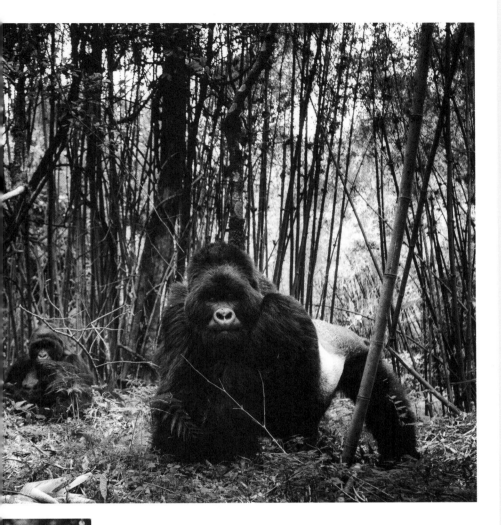

UGANDA'S BEST NATIONAL PARKS

1 **Queen Elizabeth National Park** has an unrivalled number of animal species, which includes elephants, hippos, buffalo and the rare tree-climbing lion.

2 **Murchison Falls National Park**, in northwest Uganda, is renowned for its spectacular cascades, which sees the River Nile flushed through a narrow gorge.

3 **Lake Mburo National Park** is a wetland and savannah that can be seen by 4WD and boat. Expect to see zebra, impala and waterbuck, plus hippo and crocodiles.

4 **Kibale National Park** has an evergreen rainforest and is the best place to see Uganda's primates, including chimpanzees, and red colobus and red-tailed monkeys.

5 **Rwenzori Mountains National Park** is also known as the Mountains of the Moon. The majestic range is home to snow-capped peaks and Africa's third highest mountain, Mount Stanley.

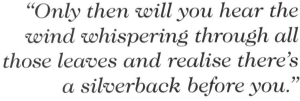

"Only then will you hear the wind whispering through all those leaves and realise there's a silverback before you."

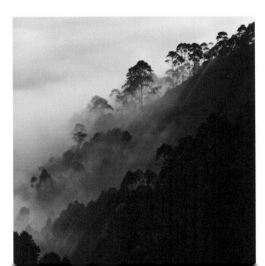

Clockwise from top Silverback mountain gorillas in the dense jungle; sunrise and mist over Bwindi's forest; a group of trekkers looking for gorillas in the canopy

TOP TIP

Travel to Uganda during the dry seasons (June–September and December–February) and you're likely to spot a variety of animals gathered around watering holes.

"A setting of incomparable beauty,
Antarctica is one of the few untouched
travel destinations left in the world."

Penguins walking on an iceberg, with the stunning blue ocean rolling below

ANTARCTICA

ANTARCTICA

WHY GO *The waters around this pristine paradise of icebergs and vast expanses of polar ice are only navigable during the summer (November–March). February is the best time to spot whales and see penguin chicks being cared for in their pebble nests.*

A setting of incomparable beauty, Antarctica is one of the few untouched travel destinations left in the world. Here, you'll spend your days cruising the frigid waves alongside humpbacks, orcas and blue whales, picking a path between aquamarine icebergs the size of ships laden with lounging fur seals. As there are no piers or docks, you'll board rubber Zodiacs (inflatable boats) when it's time to set foot on the frozen continent, where you can take in the incredible icy vistas from close quarters and get acquainted with the wildlife. In the evenings, you'll use these boats to sail up close to giant icebergs, looming from the waves in the ghostly twilight of the Antarctic summer.

Best of all are the penguins, which are found in the thousands here in Antarctica – including six varieties peculiar to the south-polar region. The birds generally hatch their eggs around December, so by February the nesting sites are a rabble of noise and activity as the chicks prepare to fledge. You'll be kept at a safe distance from nesting penguins, but many birds seem oblivious and often waddle right up to investigate – resulting in unforgettable encounters.

When Else to Go
December–January Penguin chicks start hatching and newborn seal pups appear. Temperatures are at their warmest and there's up to 20 hours of sunlight.

PLANNING YOUR TRIP Getting there Pre-booked cruises to Antarctica sail from Ushuaia, Argentina. Flights to Ushuaia depart from Buenos Aires, Argentina. **Getting around** Cruise ships enter the glacial bays and Zodiacs are used to land on the ice. **Weather** Around 18 hours of sunlight; rain and snowfall are rare. **Average temperature** 1°C / 34°F.

MIAMI

North America USA
MIAMI

WHY GO *Gorgeous swathes of sand, flamboyant Art Deco architecture, cutting-edge contemporary art and a raucous nightlife – Miami is at its best in February, with mild, dry, sunny weather. The South Beach Food & Wine Festival adds extra cachet.*

You can laze on the city's seductive beaches, dance in the moonlight or simply take in the sights and sounds of South Beach from a café on Ocean Drive – but there's much more to Miami, Florida's beating heart. Join a walking tour and admire the Art Deco hotels and condos, or paddle around the celebrity mansions of Biscayne Bay in a kayak. Sample the city's succulent stone crab claws and "Floribbean cuisine", a blend of Latin American and Caribbean flavours, before grabbing a cup of sweet Cuban coffee (*cafécito*) along Calle Ocho in Little Havana. Spend time perusing the boutiques of Coconut Grove and gallery hopping in Wynwood and the Design District. All this – and don't forget the beaches.

When Else to Go
April–May Temperatures are heating up, but the beaches are rarely crowded. Miami Beach Pride week usually takes place in April, adding plenty of colour, parades and live music.

PLANNING YOUR TRIP **Getting there** Miami Airport is linked to the centre by Metrobus, Metrorail and Tri-Rail. **Getting around** Hiring a car is the best option. South Beach and Downtown can be easily explored on foot. **Weather** Sunny and warm, with very little rainfall. **Average temperature** 24°C / 75°F.

Samba dancers
performing in the
Carnival parade,
Rio de Janeiro

South America Brazil
RIO DE JANEIRO

RIO DE JANEIRO

Art Deco
buildings on
Ocean Drive
in South
Beach, Miami

WHY GO *From the Friday before Ash Wednesday to the following Thursday, Rio de Janeiro shuts down for a week to host the world's greatest street party.*

Rio is a vast city with a mesmerizing setting, sandwiched between the balmy South Atlantic and jungle-smothered mountains. From its old Portuguese churches to its ramshackle favelas climbing the slopes at impossible angles, the city has some of the world's greatest sights. Perhaps most famous is the awe-inspiring statue of Christ the Redeemer, arms spread on iconic Sugarloaf Mountain. And let's not forget the beaches of Copacabana and Ipanema, and the Maracanã stadium, an icon to football fans.

Topping them all is Carnival, when Rio is at its most exuberant. Feathers and sequins glitter in the spotlights, massed drums boom and huge loudspeaker-laden floats tremble as thousands of dancers twist and shake to a samba beat. The main event – the procession of Grupo Especial schools known as the

Desfile – takes place in the purpose-built Sambódromo, a long concrete structure that can accommodate 90,000 spectators. Each samba school competes on the basis of song, story, dress, dance and rhythm.

There's more besides. You might stumble across an impromptu street party, day or night, with processions featuring booming samba and thousands of dressed-up revellers. Or you could visit a neighbourhood samba school, to learn how the dances and floats are put together. Then there are the wild Carnival balls and live shows – wherever you end up, it's time to join the party!

When Else to Go
December–January Reveillon (New Year's Eve) sees millions partying on Copacabana Beach.

PLANNING YOUR TRIP **Getting there** Rio Galeão Airport is connected to the city centre by taxi and express bus. **Getting around** Explore the city on foot, or use the metro or official taxis (especially at night). **Weather** Sunny and humid. Brief thunderstorms and showers likely. **Average temperature** 30°C / 86°F.

// MARCH

BARSANA, INDIA	**52**	SAN SEBASTIÁN, SPAIN	**60**
NINGALOO, AUSTRALIA	**54**	CHICAGO, USA	**62**
HIMALAYAS, NEPAL	**56**	MARRAKECH, MOROCCO	**64**
WHISTLER, CANADA	**57**	YUCATÁN, MEXICO	**66**
VALENCIA, SPAIN	**58**	ANTIGUA, GUATEMALA	**68**

Clouds circling the epic
mountains of Nepal
as the sun sets

BARSANA

Asia India
BARSANA

WHY GO *The Hindu festival of Holi sees revellers coat one another in coloured powders in honour of spring. Barsana, in north India, is unique for its legendary Lathmar Holi hilarity.*

Holi – or the "Festival of Colours" – bursts onto the Indian calendar in an explosion of colour and noise, as everyone takes to the streets with handfuls of *gulal* (coloured powder) and reckless abandon. Nothing reflects the spirit of Holi better than the rainbow powders that symbolize the change from drab winter into bright spring. *Gulal* is either used dry and smeared onto people, or mixed with water and splattered from water pistols and balloons. On the night before Holi, large *hola* (bonfires) are lit and an effigy of the demon Holika is burnt, signifying the triumph of good over evil. The mood is jubilant, but it is as dawn breaks the next day that the festival erupts.

The festival has long been presided over by Lord Krishna, whose roots in the state of Uttar Pradesh give the festivities an increased fervour in the village of Barsana. Here, Lathmar Holi follows a distinct tradition in the few days before the main Holi festival. Armed with sticks, the women make the men dress in women's clothing and dance while clouds of flame-red, turmeric-orange and electric-yellow powder cover the streets in a technicolour smog. This is a typically Indian festival, pulsing with sensuality, joy and life.

When Else to Go
October–November Diwali sees public spaces festooned with coloured lights, homes lit by clay lamps and various firework displays.

PLANNING YOUR TRIP **Getting there** Barsana is about 115 km (71 miles) southeast of Delhi, where most international flights land. **Getting around** To reach Barsana, hire a car from the airport. **Weather** March is sunny and very warm, with temperatures dropping at night. **Average temperature** 35°C / 91°F.

Right Throwing a cloud of coloured powder over revellers; a Barsana woman laughing during Lathmar Holi celebrations

Below A crowd sitting and conversing during Barsana's colour-filled festivities

NINGALOO

Oceania Australia
NINGALOO

WHY GO *Whale sharks arrive around the time of March's coral bloom, making for an incredible snorkelling experience.*

Behind the blue curtain of the deep, Ningaloo's wonders beckon. For three months of the year, the warm waters off the coast of Western Australia encounters the mighty 15-m (50-ft) whale shark, looking to feast on plankton in the March coral blooms. The whale sharks are further joined by a legion of manta rays, clownfish and starfish. Ningaloo Marine Park, stretching for 260 km (162 miles), teems with life and offers countless incredible underwater experiences. Dive at one of the world's top dive sites – Navy Pier – and watch all manner of marine life cruising the ocean floor.

When Else to Go
November This is a great time to see turtles nesting, manta rays and humpback whales.

PLANNING YOUR TRIP **Getting there** Daily flights operate to Learmonth Airport from Exmouth, the nearest town. **Getting around** A 4WD vehicle is best. **Weather** Exmouth is warm all year round with no wet season. **Average temperature** 20°C / 68°F.

Overlooking the aquamarine waters and rust-red landscape around Ningaloo Marine Park

NINGALOO DIVING SPOTS

With a wealth of marine life and coral, the Ningaloo Reef is a diver's paradise. Here are three of the best sites.

Underneath **Exmouth Navy Pier** is an astonishing underwater world. Marvel at the giant groper (*above*) and the endless numbers of colourful reef fish.

Coral gardens and swim-through caves await in the waters around the two **Muiron Islands**. Look out for sea turtles (*above*).

Dive sites in **Lighthouse Bay** feature limestone ledges and stunning coral formations. Whale sharks (*above*), pelagic fish and the rare frogfish are just some of the highlights.

HIMALAYAS

Asia Nepal
HIMALAYAS

WHY GO *The majestic Himalayas are home to nine of the world's highest mountains. Go trekking in March when it's mild and spectacular rhododendrons blanket the hillsides.*

Nepal is the crown of the Indian subcontinent, and the Himalayas, looming over the country with their snowcapped peaks, are an intrinsic part of any visit here. Of the country's mountains, Everest is, of course, the main draw, but the trek to the summit is hard work and only for the fit. There are also plenty of other trails which offer an equally thrilling experience. Passing through surprisingly lush valleys filled with wildflowers and calling into Sherpa villages along the way, you will love all that this mountain kingdom has to offer.

When Else to Go
Mid-September–November Autumn brings clear, sunny days and warm nights.

PLANNING YOUR TRIP **Getting there**
Flights arrive into Tribhuvan International Airport, not far from Kathmandu. Catch an onward flight to Lukla, the start of the trek. **Getting around** Hire a guide. Be sure you have the necessary permits. **Weather** Dry and mild but cold at higher altitudes (and at night). **Average temperature** 11°C / 52°F.

Khumbu Icefall, overlooking Everest Base Camp

Skiing through mountainside alpine forests in Whistler

WHISTLER

North America Canada
WHISTLER

WHY GO *It's all about the great outdoors in Whistler. Spring sees sunny days and powder aplenty, allowing for all manner of winter sports.*

This pretty resort village is cradled in one of the most scenic spots in western Canada. The Whistler and Blackcomb mountains dominate the landscape, with more than 200 ski runs, 16 alpine bowls and three glaciers. Quiet trails through thick forests of fragrant pine and cedar beckon cross-country skiers, while the icy surface of the frozen Green Lake seems purpose-made for ice skating. And then there's heli-skiing, snowtubing, ice climbing and so much more besides.

When you've had your fill of thrills, Whistler is a surprisingly cosmopolitan place to while away the evening. Enjoy an après-ski craft beer or cocktail at one of the many lounge bars and take in the spectacular scenery.

When Else to Go
December Plenty of Yuletide cheer, sleigh rides and an annual film festival.

PLANNING YOUR TRIP **Getting there** Flights arrive into Vancouver and a shuttle continues to Whistler. Car hire is also available. **Getting around** A free shuttle provides transport to the ski lifts. **Weather** Snowy and mild, though cold on the mountain. **Average temperature** 2°C / 36 °F.

Above Revellers dressed as devils carrying flaming torches through the city streets

Right A burning *falla* underneath an explosion of fireworks at the Fallas Festival

VALENCIA

Europe Spain
VALENCIA

WHY GO *Anarchy erupts on Valencia's streets during March's Fallas Festival, a raucous romp of giant puppets, firework displays and fiery festivities.*

Pumping out clouds of gunpowder smoke, the multitude of fireworks explodes with such ferocity that the ground judders. The explosions increase in volume until, before you know it, the ruckus stops and the crowd bursts into spontaneous applause. Today's *mascletà* – a daytime firework display – is over, and tomorrow's will probably be even louder. This is the Fallas Festival, a boisterous burst of colourful fireworks, explosions and processions in honour of St Joseph, the patron saint of carpenters.

From 15 to 19 March, more than 300 huge, elaborate papier-mâché sculptures – the *fallas* – are set up in the city streets to be inspected and judged on their artistic merit. There is an air of unruly celebration that slowly builds to a crescendo of hysteria and anarchy. Revellers are sustained by creamy hot chocolate and sugar-dusted churros, while hardcore partygoers seek stronger, around-the-clock stimulation in the many bars of the buzzing Barrio del Carmen.

On the final night, the sculptures are packed with fireworks and set alight. As the flames greedily consume each work of art, the ecstatic onlookers pull back to avoid the heat, while firefighters nonchalantly hose down nearby buildings, occasionally flicking plumes of water over the spectators. Within minutes, each sculpture, which has typically taken six months to create, has been burnt to the ground in a spectacular fiery climax of wanton destruction.

When Else to Go
July Feria de Julio is a month-long extravaganza of parades, fireworks and concerts.

PLANNING YOUR TRIP **Getting there** The city centre is accessible from Valencia Airport by bus, metro, car or taxi. **Getting around** The city centre is best explored on foot. **Weather** Valencia is pleasantly sunny in March, though it does get cooler at night. **Average temperature** 18°C / 64°C.

CITY HIGHLIGHTS

After a day of revelry, dive into the best of the city's rich cultural heritage.

Gothic architecture Valencia's historic centre is filled with a wealth of Gothic architecture. Don't miss La Lonja de la Seda, the Silk Exchange, with its soaring twisted columns and intricate vaulted ceiling *(above)*.

Street art The best of the city's street art is in Barrio del Carmen. Our favourite is Julieta XLF's colourful kawaii-inspired scenes along Calle de la Beneficencia.

Amazing museums World-class museums abound in the city. Essential viewing is the Museo Nacional de Cerámica, with its opulent alabaster façade.

Marvellous markets From street fairs to covered stalls, Valencia's markets can't be beat. Head to art nouveau Mercado Central *(below)* for foodie treats, then scour open-air Ruzafa and Rastro for vintage treasures.

SAN SEBASTIÁN

Europe Spain
SAN SEBASTIÁN

WHY GO *San Sebastián is the jewel in Spain's culinary crown, and March is a great time to quaff Basque cider and join locals on the* pintxos *trail.*

Lovers of the good things in life will feel at home in San Sebastián. One of the top culinary destinations not only in Spain but anywhere in the world, this seaside Basque city is rightly celebrated for its *pintxos* (Basque tapas), its seafood and its wine, and gourmands of all stripes pack out its backstreet tapas bars and multi-Michelin-starred restaurants. Gazing out over the Bay of Biscay with a glass of *txakoli* (sparkling wine) is an unbeatable way to pass an evening, as is the *txikiteo* – a crawl of the Parte Vieja's tapas bars, where you can sample classic dishes like salted cod, veal cheek and pickled anchovies. These are the places to tap into the rhythm of local life, particularly in the evening, when locals flood out of workplaces and into the cobbled streets. Even better, this is cider season and there are plenty of opportunities to sample this celebrated local tipple.

Beach lovers, too, love San Sebastián. Playa de la Concha sweeps in a golden arc along the city's northern edge. Named for its shell-like shape, the beach is hugged by the mountains of Urgull and Igueldo, and its sheltered waters are ideal for a dip.

Sun setting over the picturesque Playa de la Concha, San Sebastián

Any trip to San Sebastián should end with a ride on the funicular to the slopes of mighty Monte Igeldo, where a terraced lookout point is a spectacular spot to watch the sun melt into the horizon.

When Else to Go
August Semana Grande sees street parties and firework displays.
September Boat races take place in Playa de la Concha.

PLANNING YOUR TRIP **Getting there** San Sebastián Airport is east of the city centre, which can be reached by bus, car or taxi. **Getting around** San Sebastián is well connected by a bus network and cycle lanes, with various car and bike hire outlets. **Weather** Mild with some showers. **Average temperature** 14°C / 57°F.

ON THE PINTXOS TRAIL

For many, San Sebastián is synonymous with one thing: food. *Pintxos* are the Basque take on tapas, eaten over a glass of something chilled in drinking holes in lively Parte Vieja (Old Quarter), often as part of a bar crawl. Here are some typical dishes to whet your appetite.

---

1 The most famous of all Basque *pintxos*, the *Gilda* is a simple skewer of olives, peppers and anchovies – a must try for anyone on the trail.

2 *Rabas negras* is a striking take on classic calamari – fried rings of squid cooked in its own ink, lending it a deep black colour.

3 Much beloved in neighbouring Portugal, *bacalao* (salted cod) is also a long-time favourite; enjoy it skewered with peppers or deep-fried.

4 *Txuleta* is steak produced from mature, grass-fed beef. The Basques grill the beef to perfection. This is best enjoyed with a glass of red.

5 *Idiazabal* cheese is made from sheep's milk and is often served on small pieces of bread topped with quince and Iberico ham *(below)*.

CHICAGO

North America USA
CHICAGO

WHY GO *Crowds flock to Chicago's streets the weekend before St Patrick's Day (17 March) to follow joyous parades and admire the shamrock-green river at the biggest party outside of Ireland.*

Hundreds of green, white and orange flags flap in the wind; Irish dancers pound out a rhythm on the asphalt, feet flying faster than the eye can follow; the bleating of bagpipes is punctuated with the happy shouts of children; and the piercing green river flows through the joyous revelry.

It's March in the Windy City and, for one rowdy mid-month weekend, Chicago transforms into a city of *craic*. Nearly a million local residents proudly claim their heritage as Irish thanks to mid-19th-century Irish immigrants who built this city. This explains the fervour with which St Patrick's Day is celebrated here; this is, after all, the only US city to dye a river green in honour of Ireland's patron saint. Chicago hosts two grand parades on the Saturday and Sunday before the official holiday, drawing hundreds of thousands of Irish people – and Irish-for-a-day.

The Saturday parade is a family affair, while Sunday witnesses the more local South Side Irish St Patrick's Day parade in the Beverly neighbourhood, where increasingly boisterous partygoers inside the pubs can make for a more interesting show than the marching bands and floats rolling past.

Indeed, the parades are only part of the story. As early as Friday morning, revellers can already be found queuing up outside the doors of the city's Irish bars, which swell with Guinness-drinkers. Once the first parade is over, the partying truly begins, as parade spectators flood into bars, fiddlers provide a constant soundtrack and the bacchanalian mood reaches fever pitch.

When Else to Go
June Time your visit with the Chicago Blues Festival and Chicago Pride Fest, plus early summer weather.

PLANNING YOUR TRIP Getting there Most international traffic arrives at O'Hare International Airport. **Getting around** Chicago's elevated railway is an easy way to get around the city, particularly during the St Patrick's Day celebrations. **Weather** March is often overcast, rain is frequent and snow is occasional. **Average temperature** 8°C / 46°F.

Chicago's river, dyed in honour of St Patrick's Day, flowing between the city's iconic skyscrapers

PICTURE PERFECT

Marrakech's captivating colours and
golden light are a shutterbug's dream.
Here are some of the best spots.

1

As the sun sets, capture the frenetic energy of
the night market in **Jemaa el-Fna** from one
of the terraced cafés surrounding the square.

2

Ben Youssef Madrasa is a peaceful antidote
to the chaotic clammer of the medina.
Get there early to avoid the crowds.

3

For an explosion of colour, head to the
Jardin Majorelle, where vibrant blooms
contrast with intense blue backdrops.

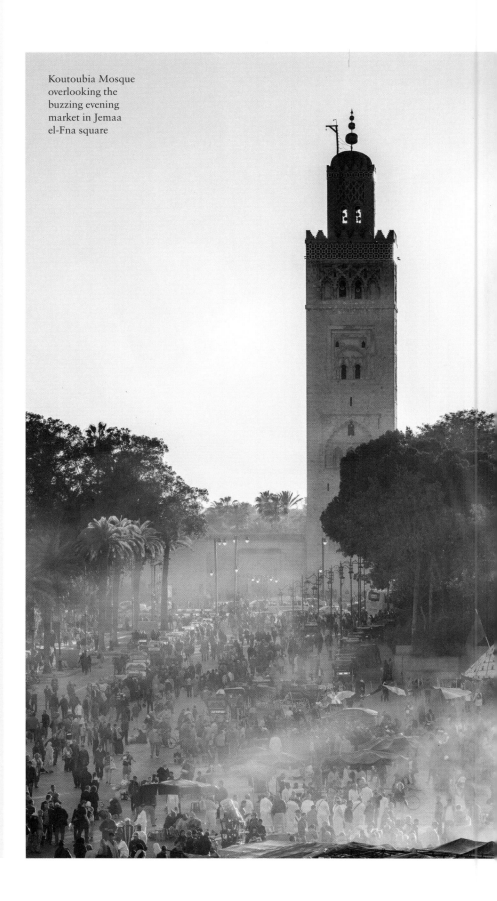

Koutoubia Mosque
overlooking the
buzzing evening
market in Jemaa
el-Fna square

MARRAKECH

Africa Morocco
MARRAKECH

WHY GO *The treasures that lie within the dusky pink medina walls of mystical Marrakech are best discovered in March, when temperatures are cooler and crowds are smaller.*

The spectacular Jemaa el-Fna, the main square in Marrakech, is the beating heart of the city, throbbing day and night with an extraordinary carnival of snake-charmers, storytellers, acrobats and musicians, all drawing enthralled crowds. In the evening, the square transforms into a giant open-air restaurant as hundreds of stalls sell traditional favourites, from delicious flame-grilled meats to *harira* (a thick lentil and chickpea soup) or – for those wishing to have a truly Moroccan experience – boiled sheep's head. Simply sit back on one of the many benches around the square and enjoy the sizzling, smoke-filled hustle and bustle of it all.

But there's more to this romantic old trading city. Head for the souks north of the square – a vast area of higgledy-piggledy cupboard-sized shops and stalls filling dozens of narrow alleyways. A delicious mix of heady aromas draws you further into the endless maze of lanes, where stalls are laden with bunches of fresh mint, jars of plump olives infused with lemon and garlic, mounds of succulent Medjool dates and bright pyramids of spices. Intricately tooled leather, metalwork, brass lanterns, carpets and jewellery are all here in abundance. Each area specializes in a particular item, so one street might be filled with colourful leather *babooshes* (slippers), the next with sparkling glazed pottery. Whether you are buying or not, it is a wholly entrancing experience.

When Else to Go
April–May Join locals for Ramadan as they break their fast in Jemaa el-Fna after sunset.
September–November Cooler temperatures make this a perfect time for sightseeing.

PLANNING YOUR TRIP **Getting there** Flights arrive into Menara International Airport. Grab a taxi (agree on a price before setting off) or catch the No 19 bus into the city. **Getting around** The city is best seen on foot or by bike but taxis come in handy when it's particularly hot. **Weather** By March the city is heating up, though temperatures drop at night. **Average temperature** 23°C / 73°F.

Pink-hued walls of Marrakech's ancient medina

YUCATÁN

Central America Mexico
YUCATÁN

WHY GO *The Descent of Kukulcán, down the northern staircase of the spectacular ancient Mayan El Castillo pyramid, can be seen from mid-February into April, but it is at its best on the spring equinox, on 20 and 21 March.*

You sit with fellow onlookers watching the spectacle, awestruck. Brilliant sunlight picks out the tail of a giant serpent carved alongside the great north staircase of El Castillo, the pyramid at the heart of the ruined Mayan city of Chichén Itzá. As the day moves on, seven triangles of light form a zigzag on the steps and bring the serpent to life. This phenomenon – the Descent of Kukulcán – happens every year on the spring equinox. Aligned with the sun and stars with amazing precision, El Castillo was built around AD 800. It has 365 steps around its four sides, one for each day of the year – effectively making it a huge clock.

When Else to Go

November The weather is dry and warm, but not sweltering, and tourists are yet to descend on the Mayan sights.

PLANNING YOUR TRIP **Getting there** Cancún Airport handles most international flights, Merida mostly domestic. **Getting around** First-class buses are a good way of getting around, but a car is useful if you want to explore more freely. **Weather** Tropical and hot, though cooler at night. **Average temperature** 31°C / 88°F.

Stunning El Castillo, sitting at the centre of the Mayan city of Chichén Itzá

ANTIGUA

Central America Guatemala
ANTIGUA

WHY GO *Holy Week is a wonderful time to visit Antigua and experience the festivities. The air is filled with fragrances and the streets are decorated with meticulous mosaic patterns.*

Lively strains of salsa and marimba music; the rhythmic pat, pat, pat of hands forming tortillas; the soft voices of Mayan ladies urging you to buy the bright woven *huipils* (blouses) that turn every market stall and courtyard into a vivid kaleidoscope – this is Antigua, Guatemala's former colonial capital, and one of the most beautiful cities in Latin America.

For one week in spring the city takes on a whole new dimension, a sense of calm overlaying its usual lively buzz as residents pause to remember the most solemn of seasons in the Christian faith: Holy Week. The largely Catholic Guatemalans devoutly decorate the paving stones of their streets with intricate mosaics of bright blossoms and coloured sawdust. Over these ephemeral carpets, robed men bear heavy statues of Christ in penance for their year's transgressions. The scene is beautiful and moving, an unselfconscious statement of faith encompassing sorrow as participants remember the Via Dolorosa – the Way of Tears that Christ travelled to Calvary – and hope for a new beginning at Easter.

There's much more to explore in Guatemala. At the other end of the country, an untamed wilderness of jungle and swamps, stretching between Mexico and Belize, awaits. Temples atop Mayan pyramids break through the lush rainforest canopy; enigmas that have confounded archaeologists since the dense coverings of vines were first torn away to reveal their stones. Once a thriving city, Tikal was abandoned a millennium ago and is remarkable for its eerie desolation. Ponder its mysteries as you wander its winding paths, greeted by the cries of tropical birds and howler monkeys in the branches overhead.

When Else to Go
December The mid-month Palo Volador celebrates the Feast of St Tomas, with bungee-like acrobats.

Right Processing alongside mosaics made from coloured sawdust on Good Friday

Below A young boy swinging burning incense before a religious float

PLANNING YOUR TRIP **Getting there** Antigua lies 26 km (16 miles) from Guatemala City, where international flights arrive at La Aurora Airport. Buses and taxis connect to Antigua. **Getting around** For Tikal, frequent flights connect Guatemala City to Flores. Transfers are included in most tours or arranged on arrival. **Weather** This is Guatemala's dry season. **Average temperature** 22°C / 72°F.

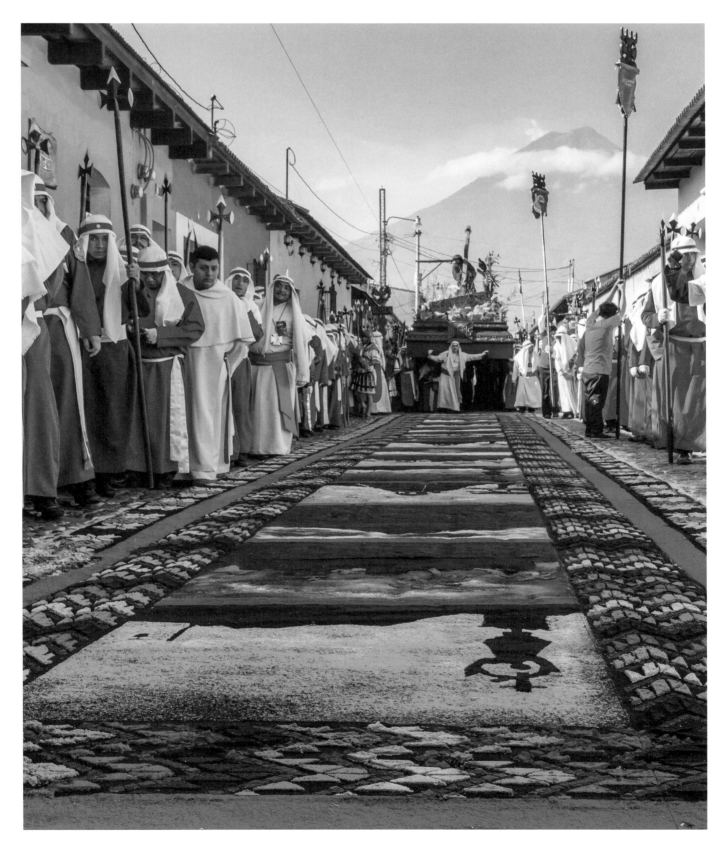

// APRIL

FJORD CRUISE, NORWAY   **72**

PETRA, JORDAN   **74**

SAMARKAND, UZBEKISTAN   **76**

BOLLENSTREEK,
THE NETHERLANDS   **78**

KYOTO, JAPAN   **80**

IGUAÇU FALLS, BRAZIL   **82**

ISTANBUL, TURKEY   **84**

GALÁPAGOS ISLANDS,
ECUADOR   **88**

PERHENTIAN ISLANDS,
MALAYSIA   **89**

ATHENS, GREECE   **90**

AMALFI COAST, ITALY   **92**

BOSTON, USA   **94**

The picture-postcard
village of Positano
clinging to the hills of
the Amalfi Coast

BERGEN

Europe Norway
FJORD CRUISE

WHY GO *Experience two seasons in one amazing voyage as you sail from Bergen, where spring is in full bloom, to Kirkenes, deep in the Arctic North.*

Norway's dramatic coastline is one of the world's natural wonders. Forested mountains stand with their feet in pristine fjords, their snowy peaks raked with cloud as waterfalls plunge into deep channels of icy water below. Nestled among them, wooden houses are painted in shades of mustard and cinnamon, briny fishing boats line pretty harbour fronts and, in the cities, ancient history sits alongside the familiar hum of 21st-century life.

Every day of the year, a Hurtigruten (Coastal Voyage) ship leaves Bergen and heads north for Kirkenes, way above the Arctic Circle. The 12-day round-trip takes in 34 ports, berthing in the craggy-peaked Lofoten Islands, the Arctic city of Tromsø and Honningsvåg, home to the fascinating North Cape Museum. The hop-on hop-off service means you can jump ashore and embark on city tours, venture into glacier country, hike steep mountain passes and encounter the Sámi way of life. This trip is truly a unique voyage of discovery.

When Else to Go
May Sleepy Bergen springs to life during Bergen International Festival, with music, ballet, theatre, dance and performing arts.

PLANNING YOUR TRIP Getting there Pre-booked cruises sail from Bergen, served by Bergen Airport, Flesland. **Getting around** Bergen Light Rail links the airport to the city. **Weather** Sunshine, rain and snow above the Arctic Circle. **Average temperature** 6°C / 43°F.

Clockwise from top left
Norwegian flag blowing in the arctic wind aboard a Norwegian cruise ship; puffin perching on a rock in Runde; the picturesque town of Hamnøy in the Lofoten archipelago

PETRA

Asia Jordan
PETRA

WHY GO *Petra's rock-hewn façades seem almost otherworldly as they reflect the swirls of colour that pattern the surrounding hillsides. April promises cool temperatures and an abundance of wild blooms – the perfect backdrop to this "rose-red city".*

The ancient Nabataean city of Petra surpasses all expectations – to call it dramatic is an understatement. This spectacular city is truly one of the world's most atmospheric ancient sites.

Leaving behind a scorched and bleak stony landscape, you enter a narrow canyon known as the Siq, squeezed between vertical rock walls that are in places so narrow you can barely see the sky. This is the secretive entrance to a city that remained hidden to the outside world for over half a millennium. Advancing along the Siq, the sense of anticipation grows, until you round the final bend and come face-to-face with the famous rose-pink façade of the Treasury, chiselled out of the solid rock wall. To the right, the canyon widens, its glowing veined walls sculpted with façades of columns, pediments and ornate doorways. A little further on stands a theatre carved deep into the hillside, and beyond, a sandy-floored main street. If that was it, it would be staggering enough, but it's not. From here you clamber up rocky staircases and passageways to yet more tombs and monuments, to the ruins of a Crusader castle, and to a great altar known as the High Place of Sacrifice, with fantastic views of the mountains and desert beyond. Petra is far more than just an archaeological site, it's a breathtaking adventure into the past.

When Else to Go
October Enjoy crisp days, cool nights and splashes of autumn colour along Petra's watercourses.

PLANNING YOUR TRIP **Getting there** Jordan's capital, Amman, is served by Queen Alia International Airport. There are regular bus connections to Petra from Amman. **Getting around** Explore the site on foot or by calèche (horse-drawn carriage). **Weather** Mild and pleasant. **Average temperature** 22°C / 71°F.

UNMISSABLE SIGHTS

This spectacular Nabatean city is home to an overwhelming array of ancient wonders. Here are a few highlights.

Built into the rose-pink rock face in the 1st century BC, the colonnaded façade of the **Treasury** is easily one of the most incredible sights in the Middle East.

A mesmerizing sight, the **Monastery** is second only to the Treasury in impact. The path to the site is carved into the mountains.

The **High Place of Sacrifice** is the best preserved of Petra's sacrificial sites. The altar at the summit is marked by two stone obelisks.

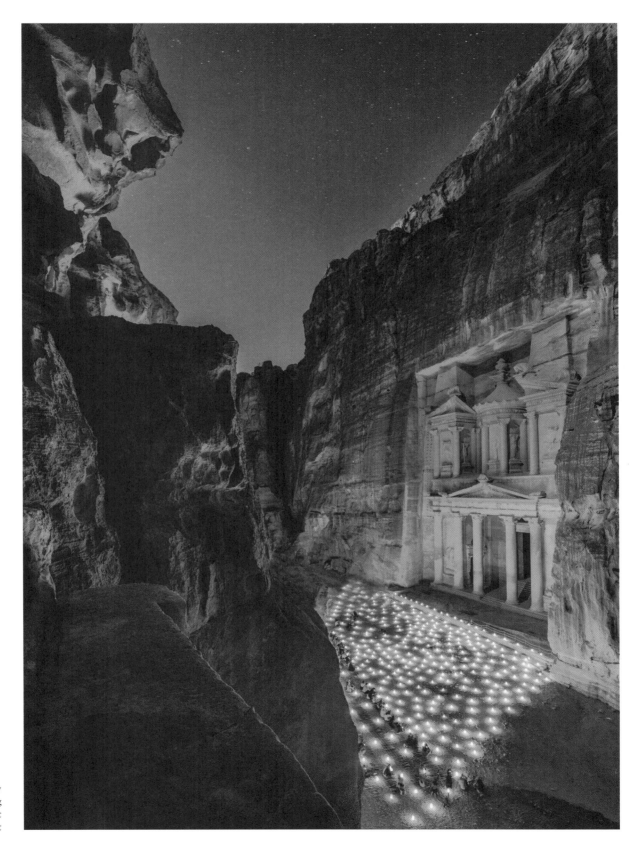

The utterly
breathtaking
Treasury, lit
by candlelight

"A golden sunlight makes everything shimmer, from tomb mosaics to vivid lapis-blue tiled cupolas."

Left Ornate mosaics adorning Samarkand's opulent Registan

Above Highly decorative ceiling in Samarkand's Shah-i-Zinda necropolis; an Uzbek man

SAMARKAND

Asia Uzbekistan
SAMARKAND

WHY GO *With its distinctive blue-tiled mosques, mausoleums and* madrassahs, *Samarkand is a glittering gem on the Silk Road. April is the perfect month to visit this scintillating city, before the extreme summer heat and sandstorms set in.*

One of the most alluring of the ancient Silk Road trading stops, Samarkand luxuriates in a golden sunlight that makes everything shimmer, from tomb mosaics and vivid lapis-blue tiled cupolas, to the gold and silver threads that run the lengths of brightly coloured fabric, silk rugs and scarves piled high in the central bazaar. Here the air is filled with the aromas of spices and *shashlik* (mutton kebabs) sizzling over hot, glowing charcoals.

Your first port of call here is the Registan – a vast square, framed on three sides by a trio of 15th- to 17th-century *madrassahs* (religious colleges). And it won't disappoint. Adorned with

delicate patterns and intricate floral, calligraphic and geometric motifs in dazzling blues, greens and golds, the scale and beauty of these buildings is breathtaking. But beyond the imposing minarets, colourful bazaars and tranquil Islamic gardens lies another side to this ancient city. Soviet-style frescoes depict scenes of the Russian Revolution, crumbling Brutalist monuments pay hommage to science and progress, and vodka is the tipple of choice – a hangover from Uzbekistan's Soviet past.

Samarkand is also an excellent base from which to explore. Drink green tea with the locals in nearby Bukhara, travel west along the Silk Road to Khiva, the

last outpost before the desert, or head south to trek the high ground of the picturesque Aman Kutan Mountains.

When Else to Go
October The temperature is pleasant and autumnal light illuminates the blue-glazed tiles of the city's buildings.

PLANNING YOUR TRIP
Getting there International flights arrive in Samarkand International Airport. High-speed rail links run from the capital, Tashkent. **Getting around** Buses are cheaper and more frequent than trains. **Weather** Sunny; rain is unusual. **Average temperature** 22°C / 72°F.

BOLLENSTREEK

Europe The Netherlands
BOLLENSTREEK

WHY GO *Late springtime in the Bollenstreek, the Netherlands' "Garden of Eden", is bursting and beautiful with the world's greatest flower spectacle.*

The moment you arrive in the Bollenstreek, a bulb-growing district famous for its vast fields of petal-perfect tulips, plus freesias, hyacinths and daffodils, you'll understand why the Netherlands is the world's greatest bloom exporter. Beginning in January, the flowering season peaks in late spring with the arrival of late-blooming lilies and – the show-stealer – fields covered by millions of tulips erupting in a rainbow of colours.

Most tulip tours of the region start in the charismatic city of Haarlem, the northernmost point of the Dutch flower empire. From here the Bollenstreek stretches southwards for 40 km (25 miles), providing plenty of opportunity for you to soak up the perfumes and natural theatre of springtime. For many, the undoubted highlight of the region is the Keukenhof, the celebrated flower garden of Lisse, which opened in 1949 and has some 17 km (10 miles) of pathways carpeted with row upon row of flowerbeds.

When Else to Go
February–March Crocuses and snowdrops are in full bloom, hailing the end of winter.

PLANNING YOUR TRIP **Getting there** Haarlem is served by Schiphol Airport. There are regular trains from Amsterdam. **Getting around** Hire a car or a bike and cycle between fields; everything is well signposted. **Weather** Sunshine is common, as are light showers. **Average temperature** 13°C / 55°F.

Left Row upon row of flowering tulips in the Bollenstreek

Below The charming waterside city of Haarlem, the starting point of trips to the Bollenstreek

KYOTO

Asia Japan
KYOTO

WHY GO *Kyoto comes alive in spring as cherry blossoms burst into bloom, creating a magical backdrop to this enchanting city. The custom of blossom-viewing – or* hanami *– is unmissable.*

Ancient Kyoto is the yin to modern Tokyo's yang, a city where elegance and philosophy permeate every aspect of daily life. Home to an impressive 17 UNESCO World Heritage Sites – 13 Buddhist temples, three Shinto shrines and the romantic Nijo Castle – Kyoto is, unarguably, the bastion of Japan's rich cultural landscape.

Springtime is awaited in Japan with keen anticipation; the meteorological agency even monitors the so-called "cherry blossom front" allowing the public to follow the flowering trees during the *sakura* (cherry blossom) season. In Kyoto, parks, temples and public spaces are dusted with delicate pink and white blossoms, and the cultural events held throughout *hanami* are unparalleled. This is the perfect time to join the many who stroll along the Philosopher's Path – a pleasant canal-side trail lined by cherry trees that winds its way through Kyoto's Higashiyama district from Kiyomizu-dera Temple to Ginkaku-ji (the Silver Pavilion).

Beyond the blooms, Kyoto is known for its association with geisha (or *geiko* in the local dialect), the "arts person" who makes her home in one of Kyoto's *hanamachi* (flower towns). The geisha stage special cherry dances throughout the month of April, the most famous of which is the Miyako Odori, or "capital city dance", so named because Kyoto was once the imperial capital of Japan. The revered geisha and *maiko* (geisha in training) of the Gion Kobu perform their captivating art with grace and skill.

When Else to Go
November Enjoy blazing autumnal colours during the *koyo* (autumn leaf viewing) season.

PLANNING YOUR TRIP

Getting there Kyoto is served by Kansai International Airport, and is also around 2½ hours from Tokyo by bullet train. **Getting around** The city has a small subway system and bus network. **Weather** Sunny and mild. **Average temperature** 20°C / 68°F.

Right Traditional Japanese kimono textile; the striking Fushimi Inari Taisha at the base of Mount Inari

Below Sunset at Kiyomizu-dera Temple during the *sakura* season

IGUAÇU FALLS

South America Brazil
IGUAÇU FALLS

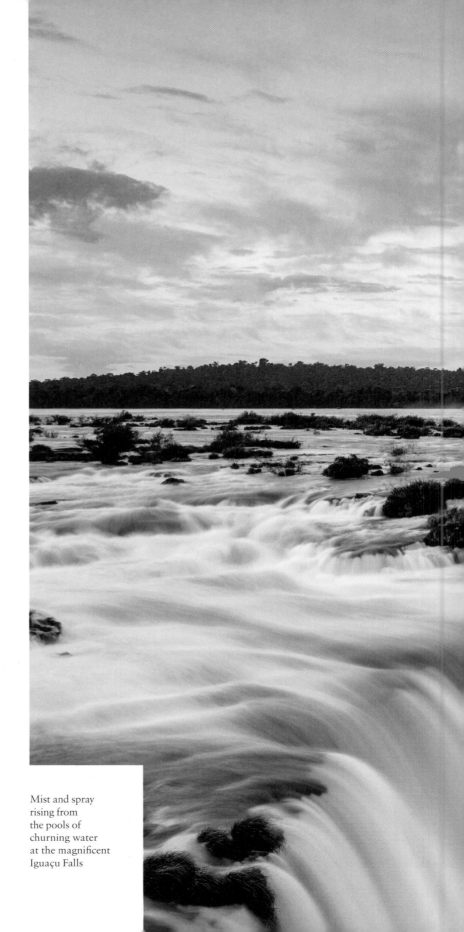

WHY GO *A thunderous display of the power of nature, the Iguaçu Falls are at their most dramatic in April, when they are swollen with summer rainfall.*

No waterfall on earth can match Iguaçu's combination of towering heights, soul-churning flow and pristine rainforest setting. The falls straddle the border between southern Brazil and northern Argentina, where the powerful but slow-moving Iguaçu River splits and tumbles over a 3-km- (2-mile-) wide precipice, hurtling into the swirling waters of the cavernous gorge below with a deafening roar. Here, hundreds of perfect rainbows form in mist that hovers above the frothing water.

Experience the falls from a boat at the bottom of the cascade, or on foot, from distant vantage points with long, sweeping vistas and on viewing platforms, where the falls' cool spray will soak you in a matter of seconds.

When Else to Go
August–September Water levels drop, revealing hidden rock formations behind the falls.

PLANNING YOUR TRIP **Getting there** The nearest city, Foz do Iguaçu, is a two-hour flight from Rio de Janeiro and São Paulo. **Getting around** Buses, taxis and tourist vans ferry visitors around. **Weather** Clear and dry. **Average temperature** 18°C / 64°F.

Mist and spray rising from the pools of churning water at the magnificent Iguaçu Falls

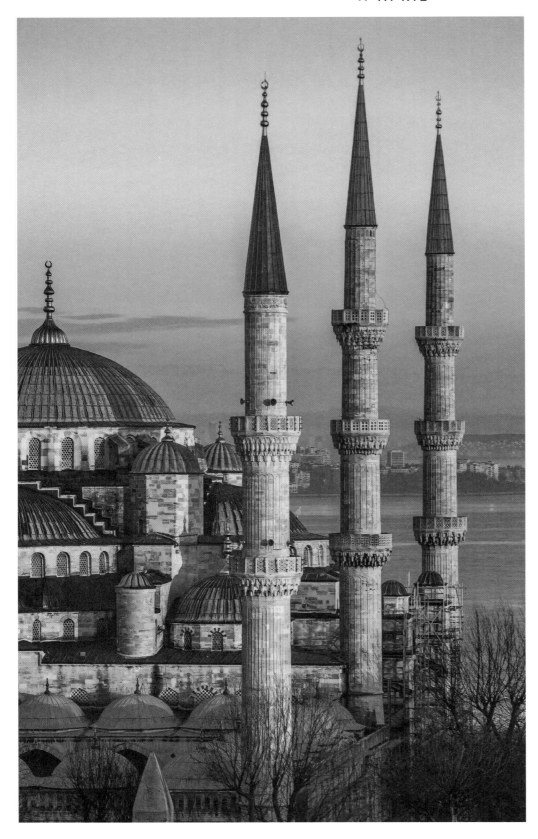

Istanbul's iconic
Blue Mosque, one
of the most majestic
mosques in Turkey

ISTANBUL

Asia/Europe Turkey
ISTANBUL

WHY GO *Spring brings new energy to Istanbul. Before crowds arrive en masse and summer heat sets in, April is the perfect time to discover all that this cosmopolitan city has to offer.*

Istanbul, with its beautiful spiky skyline of delicate minarets and onion domes, is a city adorned with fantastic palaces decorated with riches gained in conquest. The city's roots as an ancient trading post are evident in the Grand Bazaar, with its covered passageways and glittering stalls. Here, you can lose yourself for hours.

A short stroll downhill brings you to the waters of the Golden Horn, spanned by the Galata Bridge that links the old city with the new. The main street, Istiklal Caddesi, and its network of tiny lanes are a cluster of boutiques, cafés, restaurants, bars and clubs. It's here that you'll find creamy *tarama*, the best food in town, plus mussels stuffed with rice and spices, the obligatory kebab, and, of course, all manner of mouthwatering meze.

As a former capital of two major empires – the ancient Byzantine and the Ottoman Turkish – Istanbul is rich with imperial history, and the architecture that goes with it. The promontory of land known today as Sultanahmet was developed under centuries of emperors and sultans – its great walls enclosed long-since vanished palaces and some of the world's earliest Christian religious establishments. Today, among the many archaeological treasures, you can explore the magnificent Topkapı Palace, the Blue Mosque and the remnants of the great hippodrome that was used for chariot races.

When Else to Go
October Istanbul's parks and gardens are ablaze with autumnal colours.

PLANNING YOUR TRIP **Getting there** Istanbul is served by Atatürk and Sabiha Gokcen international airports, with bus connections to Taksim Square. **Getting around** Most sights are within walking distance from one another, but there is also a large network of tram and metro lines, and plenty of taxis. **Weather** Days are clear and mild. **Average temperature** 16°C / 61°F.

FESTIVALS AND EVENTS

Istanbul loves a party. From May to September the city comes alive with all manner of exciting summer festivals, but April features an impressive line up with a much more local feel.

Tulip Festival Turkey's national flower is the tulip *(above)*. Every April millions of bulbs bloom across the city. Roadside verges are a riot of colour, but the flowers are best viewed in parks such as Emirgan and Gülhane.

Sokak Festivali Live music, entertainment, sport and street food converge during this three-day street festival. Expect performances from the most popular musicians in the city and an eclectic mix of genres, from Balkan beats to funk, soul reggae to electronica.

International Istanbul Film Festival Film buffs descend on Istanbul at the beginning of April. Since its inception in 1982, this festival *(below)* has screened over 3,000 films from 76 countries. Most showings are held in cinemas around Istiklal Caddesi.

Süleymaniye Mosque
overlooking Istanbul's
energetic harbour

South America Ecuador
GALÁPAGOS ISLANDS

WHY GO *The Galápagos offer the most incredible eye-to-eye encounters with wildlife. In April the islands' air and sea temperatures are perfect for enjoying a dip.*

GALÁPAGOS ISLANDS

ECUADOR

This volcanic archipelago is home to a menagerie of exotic creatures. The islands, which owe their unique quality to their isolation, were set aside as a national park in 1959, and visits here are regulated so as to protect the natural residents. A licensed guide accompanies each cruise boat to enforce park rules and educate tourists on the ecology.

Join a boat excursion and watch as manta rays glide under your vessel, and bottlenose dolphins break the water's surface beside you. Dive in to join them, or the hammerhead sharks off Bartolomé Island, or sea lions in the waters around San Cristóbal Island. You can even snorkel with penguins off Fernandina. Go ashore to see the islands' namesake, the giant tortoise (*Galápago* is Spanish for tortoise), heaving its 275 kg (610 lb) weight up the beach.

Everywhere you turn, the islands' residents dance, dart and dive – this is Eden for wildlife.

When Else to Go
June–August Blue-footed boobies perform their distinctive mating rituals.

PLANNING YOUR TRIP **Getting there** International flights arrive into Quito and Guayaquil, Ecuador. From there, catch a flight to Santa Cruz. **Getting around** Small ships and charter boats offer organized outings. **Weather** Pleasantly warm with some rain. **Average temperature** 27°C / 81°F.

Two Galápagos sea lions playing in a cove off San Cristóbal Island

Clear blue waters
and bobbing boats
off the shore of one
of the delightful
Perhentian Islands

PERHENTIAN
ISLANDS

Asia Malaysia
PERHENTIAN ISLANDS

WHY GO *With warm weather and stunning scenery, the Perhentians are perfect for a relaxing spring break.*

Welcome to the world of rainforests and coral reefs – two extraordinarily diverse natural habitats. The Perhentians comprise two main islands in the South China Sea, Perhentian Besar and Perhentian Kecil, with a peppering of smaller islands nearby. Lush rainforests are protected here by unending sandy beaches, lined with swaying palms.

Quite simply, this is paradise, one where you can spend hours watching nesting turtles, scuba diving above colourful carpets of coral and mesmerizing fish, partying on the sandy beaches until sunrise or lying swinging in a hammock. These islands have it all and, for a while at least, you can forget the world you left behind.

When Else to Go
May–July Experience peak turtle-nesting season on the islands.

PLANNING YOUR TRIP **Getting there** The nearest international airport is in Kuala Lumpur. Fly on to Kota Bharu or Kuala Terengganu and catch a bus to Kuala Besut – boats run to the Perhentians from here. **Getting around** A water taxi allows you to island-hop. **Weather** Expect sunny weather. **Average temperature** 31°C / 88°F.

ATHENS

Europe Greece
ATHENS

WHY GO *Dynamic and diverse, crumbling structures and contemporary sights live cheek-by-jowl in Athens. If this heady mix isn't enough, the Greeks embrace Easter with great fervour at this time of year.*

Greece's capital is nothing short of captivating. The historic centre is an open museum, with a treasure trove of ruins and Byzantine churches sitting alongside apartment buildings and office blocks. Atop the imposing Acropolis is the majestic Parthenon – the symbol of the city. This titanic temple watches over the likes of the Ancient Agora, the Theatre of Dionysus and the Sanctuary of Zeus, plus the Greek people milling about in the cobbled streets, as they did thousands of years ago. Today, though, the view also takes in striking street art, myriad bookshops and cute cafés around every corner.

If you're in Athens at Easter *(Pascha)*, you're in for an extra treat. Holy Week begins on the Monday before Easter with a strict fast, and houses traditionally get their yearly whitewash. On Good Friday, church bells toll eerily all day, and at around 8pm candlelit processions wind slowly through the streets. At midnight on Saturday, locals meet outside churches with candles and watch fireworks. Celebrations culminate on Easter Sunday, with music resounding through the streets and the aroma of lamb from rooftop spit-roasts permeating the air.

When Else to Go
August Ancient sites stay open for the full moon. **September** Athens Classic Marathon is based on the original route from Greek legend.

PLANNING YOUR TRIP **Getting there** Athens International Airport is about 45 minutes by taxi from the centre. There's also a metro link which takes 40 minutes. **Getting around** Sights are closely packed and easily walkable, though there are also buses and a useful metro system. **Weather** Sunny and pleasant. **Average temperature** 20°C / 68°F.

Above The Parthenon atop the Acropolis, overlooking the city rooftops

Right Freshly baked *simit*; the crumbling columns of the Parthenon; *Believe in Dreams* by Wild Drawing

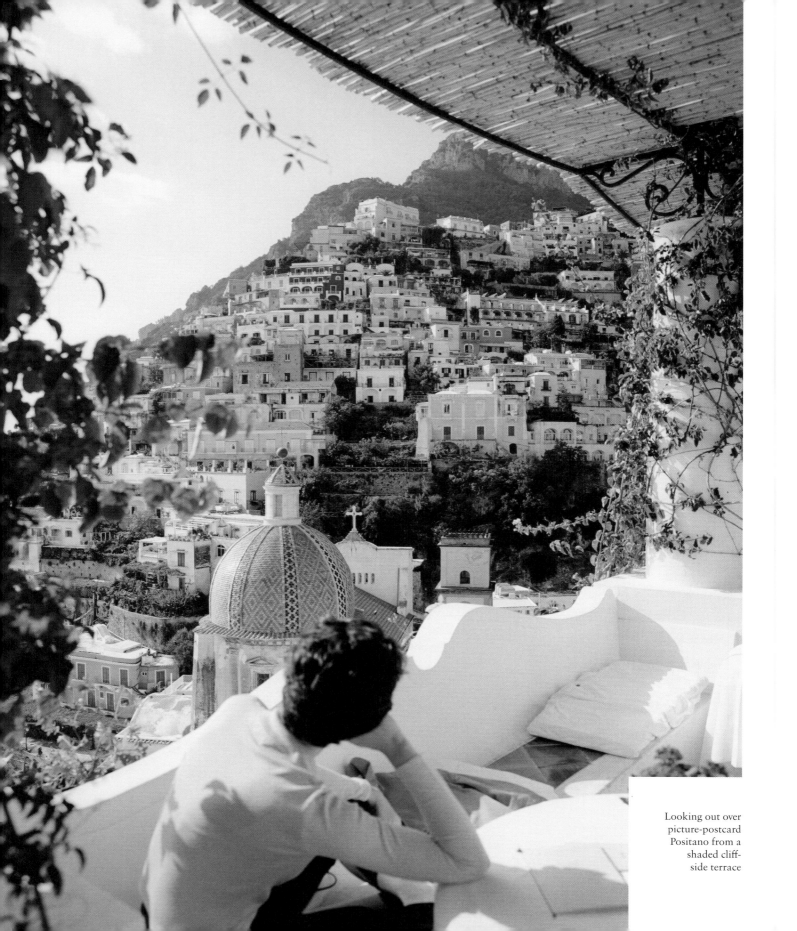

Looking out over
picture-postcard
Positano from a
shaded cliff-
side terrace

Indulgence is intrinsic to Italy and the Amalfi Coast produces the country's best lemons and seafood.

1

Delizie al Limone are sponge cakes filled with lemon cream and sealed with a zesty glaze. Their name translates as "lemon delights".

2

Fresh seafood appears in various dishes, such as local favourite *polipetti affogati* – octopus "drowned" in tomatoes and wine.

3

Limoncello is a zingy lemon-based liquor, best enjoyed in a frosted glass paired with a sea view. The perfect end to a day of driving.

AMALFI COAST

Europe Italy
AMALFI COAST

WHY GO *A drive along the Amalfi Coast is best enjoyed in April, when villages shake off their winter slumber, sun-warmed lemons hang plump and heavy, and the scent of citrus blossom lingers.*

The scenery gradually unfolds before you: towering cliffs plunge into the sea, azure waters pan out to the horizon and villages cling to the craggy mountainside. Leaving behind gritty Naples and the ancient ruins of Pompeii and Herculaneum, your journey begins in earnest, wriggling along the Sorrento Peninsular, a cliff-edged promontory of sheer rugged beauty. Sorrento, the gateway to the Amalfi Coast, sits amid terraced lemon groves that, come April, are thick with fruit. The road then sweeps across the headland before gliding up the underbelly of the peninsular and its scattering of sandy coves, signalling your arrival at Positano. The Amalfi Coast's fashionable darling is an unmissable stop: a dramatic cascade of peach, cream and blush buildings housing boutiques and eateries, tumbling to meet a crescent bay. From Positano the road continues, its folds hitching up the whitewashed beauty of Praiano and scenic Amalfi. Yet it's the final stretch of road, from Amalfi to Salerno, that holds the most stunning scenery. Here dramatic gorges and emerald caves pass by as the road climbs heavenwards to the garden-draped terraces and poised cliffside villas of Ravello. It's clear you've saved the best till last.

When Else to Go
September Summer lingers, keeping things warm, and most of the crowds have returned home, leaving the roads and towns much quieter.

PLANNING YOUR TRIP **Getting there** Naples Airport is the nearest to the coast. **Getting around** A hire car is the best way to explore the Amalfi Coast. **Weather** Days are sunny and warm with some showers. Temperatures dip at night. **Average temperature** 16°C / 61°F.

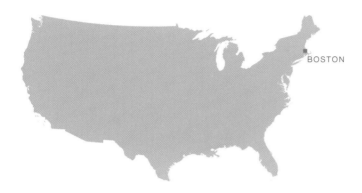

BOSTON

North America USA
BOSTON

WHY GO *With the start of the baseball season, the Boston Marathon, and basketball and ice hockey games in full swing, this is the month to join the crowds of adoring sports fanatics in Massachusetts' enigmatic capital.*

Historic and homely, Boston is a city of quiet charm and tradition but the revolutionary citadel positively pulses in April, as fans descend on Bean Town for a month of all-American sports. From early April, crowds fill out the iconic Fenway Park stadium to support the beloved Red Sox, the metallic smack of baseball bats against balls punctuating the jeers of the devoted crowds. Basketball buffs, meanwhile, watch the Boston Celtics dribble their way around the impressive TD Garden, a space shared with the Boston Bruins ice hockey team. Even those who don't enjoy competitive sports will find it hard to resist the inspiring sight of 30,000

dedicated runners pounding the city streets for the Boston Marathon on the third Monday of the month.

Sports aside, Boston's pretty neighbourhoods cry out to be explored. The townhouses and cobbled streets of Beacon Hill, topped with gas-lit Louisburg Square, are the perfectly preserved Boston of the 1840s. Sculls and sailboats glide by on the Charles River, joggers and skaters puff past on the Esplanade, and students make the place a lively city of eternal youth, filled with cafés, quirky bookshops and fashion boutiques. A visit to the city wouldn't be complete without frequenting the city's pubs, including Cheers on Beacon Hill, which inspired the TV

series of the same name. After a few nights enjoying traditional hospitality you'll relish the fresh sea breezes afforded by some New England island hopping.

When Else to Go
September Food festivals and autumn colours galore. **December** Quieter, chillier and festive.

PLANNING YOUR TRIP **Getting there** Logan International Aiport is 5 km (3 miles) from the city centre. **Getting around** Boston is compact and walkable, but you can also use the MBTA subway. **Weather** Warm and pleasant. **Average temperature** 17°C / 63°F.

Clockwise from top
Attractive townhouses
and trees lining Mount
Vernon Street, Beacon Hill;
sun rising over Fenway Park;
Hanley Ramirez batting for
the Boston Red Sox

// MAY

LAKE DISTRICT, ENGLAND   **98**

PRAGUE, CZECH REPUBLIC   **100**

LA PAZ, BOLIVIA   **101**

VICTORIA FALLS,
ZAMBIA AND ZIMBABWE   **102**

BALI, INDONESIA   **104**

WEST COAST, SCOTLAND   **106**

COLORADO PLATEAU, USA   **108**

CRETE, GREECE   **110**

SILK ROAD, CHINA   **112**

NEW YORK CITY, USA   **114**

Boats moored on the
ethereal Lake Windermere
in England's Lake District

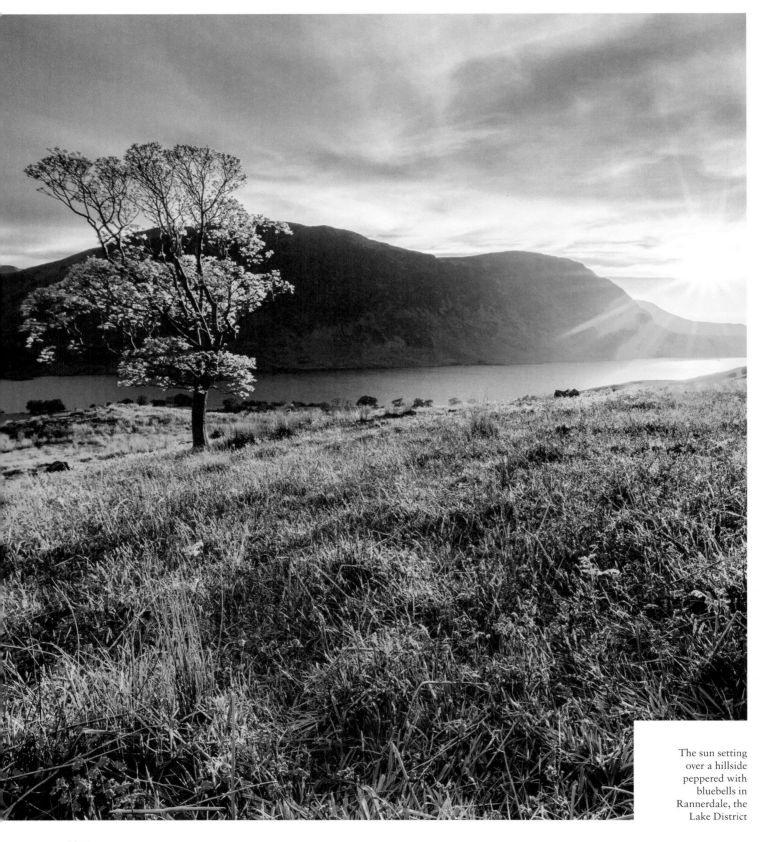

The sun setting over a hillside peppered with bluebells in Rannerdale, the Lake District

LAKE DISTRICT

Europe England
LAKE DISTRICT

WHY GO *May brings longer, milder days and an abundance of wildlife to the Lake District. Get your walking boots on and follow bluebell trails, amble through fields of frolicking lambs and climb the region's famous fells.*

Spring is in full bloom in the Lake District, a region famous for its wild, natural beauty. The landscape was immortalized in the works of William Wordsworth and Beatrix Potter, and today draws walkers looking to climb the likes of Scafell Pike, the highest summit in England at 978 m (3,210 ft).

For a trail less travelled, consider the 6-km (4-mile) stretch from Rannerdale to Buttermere, which is doable in just three hours. Following a series of paths, you'll catch sight of the region's native Herdwick sheep and smatterings of bluebells in the fields at this time of year. Rannerdale Knotts stands at 355 m (1,165 ft), making for a relatively easy ascent. As you wind your way through the lowland valleys, craggy fells rise above you, splashed with burnt orange, emerald green

and earthy brown hues. The path is a little steep towards the top of Rannerdale Knotts, so pause on a boulder and listen to the streams trickling down the hillsides and the distant trills of bleating lambs. Continue on to the peak where you're well rewarded with beautiful views out over the North Western Fells.

You've earned a hearty meal after all that walking. Follow the path back down to the village of Buttermere and tuck into lunch at one of the historic pubs. By the end of the route, you'll have experienced spring in all its glory.

When Else to Go
July–August Summer welcomes agricultural shows and beer festivals.
November Join the locals in towns and villages for Bonfire Night.

PLANNING YOUR TRIP **Getting there** The Lake District is in the northeastern county of Cumbria. There are regular trains from London Euston to Oxenholme, and from here you can get a train on to larger towns. **Getting around** A car is strongly advised. Walking and cycling are great ways to explore. **Weather** Days are generally dry, though layers are recommended as it can be brisk. **Average temperature** 12°C / 54°F.

BEST PLACES TO RECHARGE

The English countryside springs to life in May. After a day spent embracing the great outdoors, indulge in some well-earned rest and relaxation.

Ambleside Wind down in style in Zeffrelli's, a Mediterranean-inspired restaurant and jazz bar that even has its own independent cinema – opt for the meal-and-film combination and sink into those plush red seats.

Coniston Away from Coniston's Yewdale Fells is Yew Tree Farm, a quaint B&B where Beatrix Potter resided during the 1930s. Soak up the ambience in the outdoor hot tub.

Windermere Go glamping in Windermere's stunning Low Wray. At this National Trust-owned campsite, you can rest in a fully furnished safari tent or curl up in a luxury treetop pod.

Cartmel For a spot of afternoon tea, head to Cartmel's award-winning Hazelmere Café. There's a strong focus on using local produce, from Cumberland sausages to Morecambe Bay shrimps.

Grasmere Sample world-famous Grasmere gingerbread *(below)* at the 1854-established Grasmere Gingerbread Shop, before visiting William Wordsworth's grave.

PRAGUE

Europe Czech Republic
PRAGUE

WHY GO *By day, enjoy the city sights, by night, the Prague Spring concerts: this really is the best time to visit.*

Mozart once said, "My orchestra is in Prague", and during the city's legendary Spring music festival it appears that every great orchestra in the world has joined it. Since 1946 the festival has hosted only the world's very best performance artists, symphony orchestras and chamber music ensembles, all performing in Prague's first-rate venues.

The finest of the lot is the Obecní Dům (Municipal House), completed in 1911: a concert hall, ballroom, café and restaurant with such a whimsical and exuberant design that the 15th-century Powder Gate next to it appears almost offended at the flamboyant upstart. In the Smetana Hall, at the building's core, the ornate decoration leaves the concert-goer breathless and doubtful that any performer could live up to such surroundings. Time and again, however, conductors and soloists find themselves inspired to outdo the setting. It is this mix that produces arguably the greatest series of annual concerts in Europe.

When Else to Go
December Wrap up warm and get festive at Prague's wonderful Christmas markets.

PLANNING YOUR TRIP **Getting there** Václav Havel Airport is 10 km (6 miles) from the centre. **Getting around** Prague's compact centre suits walking but there is a reliable bus and tram network. **Weather** Usually sunny with minimal rainfall. **Average temperature** 18°C / 64°F.

South America Bolivia
LA PAZ

LA PAZ

WHY GO *May is an ideal time to visit La Paz and its surrounds as the weather is pleasant and mild.*

Thanks to the altitude and spectacular setting of Bolivia's de facto capital city, those arriving by air will enjoy a breathtaking introduction to La Paz. The international airport sits on the lung-stifling 4,000-m- (13,125-ft-) high Altiplano, the windswept plain that dominates southwestern Bolivia.

While the altitude, elevation and crowds make La Paz physically challenging to explore on foot, there's no better way to immerse yourself in the sights, sounds and smells of this distinctly Andean metropolis. Over half the city's population is of Aymara or Quechua heritage, and *cholas* – indigenous women wearing long plaits and clad in bowler hats and multi-layered dresses – crowd the bustling footpaths, street corners and local markets, selling everything from *empanadas* to local medicine. "*Comprame*" (buy from me), they call out to shoppers threading through the maze of vendors, hoping to engage them in a session of spirited haggling.

Accompanied by the incessant din of horn-blaring traffic, this scene is the essence of the La Paz experience – but respite isn't far. There are plenty of quiet coffee shops and diverse museums, and the city's spectacular hinterlands offer even greater scope for relaxation.

When Else to Go
June Celebrate Aymara New Year on the winter solstice.

PLANNING YOUR TRIP **Getting there** La Paz is served by El Alto International Airport. **Getting around** Travel by inexpensive taxi, *trufi* (collective taxis), *colectivos* (collective minibuses) and *micros* (buses). **Weather** Dry, mild days and cool evenings. **Average temperature** 18°C / 60°F.

Two women, dressed in traditional clothing, outside a market in La Paz

Wandering across Charles Bridge to St Vitus's Cathedral as evening settles in Prague

ZAMBIA

VICTORIA
FALLS

ZIMBABWE

Africa Zambia and Zimbabwe
VICTORIA FALLS

WHY GO *Victoria Falls is a year-round destination but May is the perfect month to come. The summer rains are over but the falls are at full flow, with rainbows common.*

Undoubtedly one of the world's great natural wonders, there's nothing to prepare visitors for the majesty of Victoria Falls, or Mosi-oa-Tunya ("the smoke that thunders"). At their widest, the falls measure over 1,700 m (5,578 ft) and at their highest 108 m (355 ft) – the largest in the world, almost twice as wide and deep as North America's Niagara.

Victoria Falls, named by David Livingstone after the Queen of the United Kingdom, straddles an international border and demonstrates two distinct personalities. In Zimbabwe, the falls remain at a distance, viewed across the gorge from a lush rainforest park created by the perpetually thick mist that's pumped out by the falling water. A more intimate relationship with the falls is available on the Zambian side. Here, visitors can saunter right up to the lip where the Zambezi plunges over the edge, or negotiate a series of mist-soaked trails and catwalks.

This contrasting nature is also evident in the two border towns. Although Zimbabwe's

reputation has suffered, Victoria Falls town thrives regardless of the country's economic and political troubles. Saturated with hotels, guesthouses, steak joints, casinos and tour agencies, it is fuelled by tourism. Zambia, meanwhile, is enjoying the fruits of its political reforms, and is fast developing a tourist scene of its own – with less of the commercialism evident across the border.

Whichever side you choose, once you've seen the falls, there's still plenty to do. Get soaked on a raft trip through the gorges or a microlight flight through the mist; enjoy a cruise on the hippo- and croc-infested river. Photograph elephants, antelope and lions on a safari; try rock-climbing; or just relax with a cold Zambezi Lager and toast the good fortune that brought you to Africa.

When Else to Go
September Come when the waters are lower to swim in the ultimate infinity pool, the Devil's Pool, with views over the waterfall's edge.

PLANNING YOUR TRIP **Getting there** Fly into Victoria Falls or Harry Mwanga Nkumbula International airports. **Getting around** Taxis from either side of the falls will get you to the respective border posts; the no-man's land between the two posts requires a walk or change of taxi. **Weather** Warm and sunny. **Average temperature** 28°C / 82°F.

"Undoubtedly one of the world's great natural wonders, there's nothing to prepare visitors for the majesty of Victoria Falls."

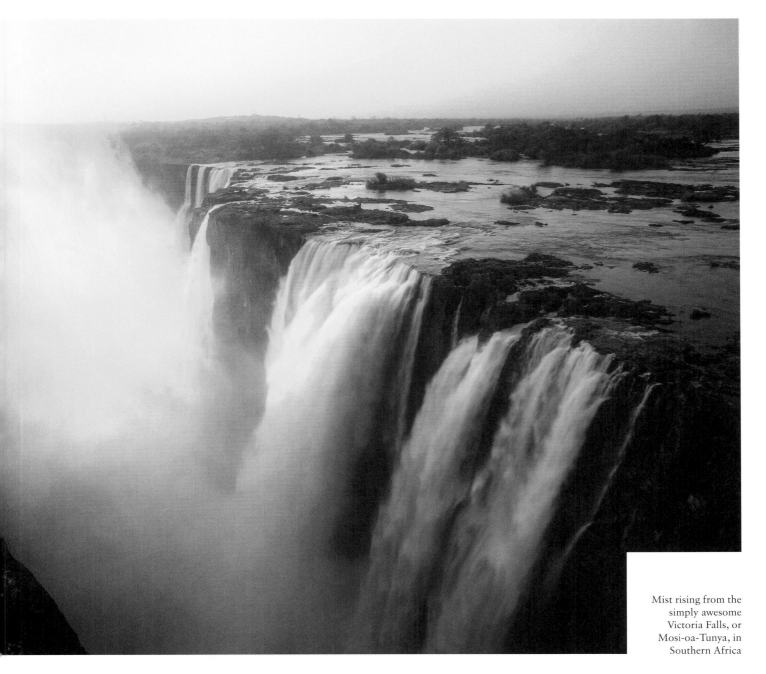

Mist rising from the simply awesome Victoria Falls, or Mosi-oa-Tunya, in Southern Africa

BALI

Right The lush rice terraces of Tegallalang, in central Bali, viewed from the air

Below A bowl of healthy fruits for breakfast; meditating by a swimming pool at sunset

Asia Indonesia
BALI

WHY GO *May brings clear skies and welcome respite from the tropical storms of Bali's rainy season. Visit in May, too, to avoid the summer crowds.*

The island of Bali, nestled within the Indonesian Archipelago, is one of the world's most relaxing holiday destinations. Exotic and diverse, the island is picturesque to the point of resembling a painted backdrop – volcanoes climb into clouds and terraced rice fields cascade down to the ocean. Bali blends its beautiful nature with a mind-bogglingly impressive concentration of spas. These spas – timeless havens of serenity – are dedicated not only to pampering the body but also to restoring inner equilibrium, and are therefore a magnet for those in search of something that will ease fatigue, stimulate the senses and awaken the spirit. Here, you can practise yoga, soothe tired muscles with a traditional Boreh treatment or simply switch off from it all and relax in near paradise.

When Else to Go
June–July Time your visit with the much celebrated Bali Arts Festival to see dance shows, concerts, art exhibitions and more.

PLANNING YOUR TRIP **Getting there** Bali is served by Ngurah Rai International Airport (Denpasar). **Getting around** Use air-conditioned taxis or hire a vehicle with a driver, or your own car or motorcycle. **Weather** May comes early in Bali's dry season. Expect sunshine, though the mountainous regions can be cooler. **Average temperature** 30°C / 86°F.

Left A picture-postcard cottage in Glencoe, west Scotland

Below Getting up close to a Highland cow; an actor dressed as Robert Burns standing outside the cottage where the poet was born

FIRTH OF CLYDE

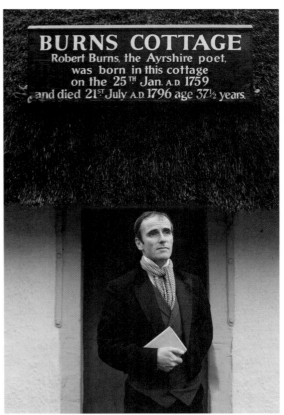

BURNS COTTAGE
Robert Burns, the Ayrshire poet, was born in this cottage on the 25TH Jan. A.D 1759 and died 21ST July A.D 1796 age 37½ years.

Europe Scotland
WEST COAST

WHY GO *Festival season hits west Scotland, with the biggest celebrations taking place during Burns An' A' That!*

The sun sinks slowly to the horizon, a golden red orb lighting liquid gold ripples across the darkening Firth of Clyde. As it disappears behind the islands and the glow fades, the night sky is suddenly alive with a brilliance of colour. People crowd onto Ayr's Low Green while others line the promenade along the beach, enjoying the fireworks and the music that is the finale of the Burns An' A' That! festival, a celebration of the life and works of Scotland's most famous poet, Robert Burns, as well as a showcase for contemporary Scottish culture. For ten days, the country has been awash with readings, tastings, concerts, walks and storytelling. If Burns were alive today there is no doubt he would be among the musicians in the pubs, swapping stories and joining the crowds for the fireworks.

Once the celebrations are over, make your way up the west coast. Wind your way past tiny picturesque fishing villages and spectacular dramatic glens, savouring undisturbed views that might inspire you to write some poetry of your own.

When Else to Go
September–October The departure of the summer crowds and the changing colours of the landscape herald a new season.

PLANNING YOUR TRIP **Getting there** Ayr is 60 km (37 miles) southwest of Glasgow, accessible via Glasgow International Airport. **Getting around** The practical way to tour the west is by car. **Weather** Wet and mild with sunny days. **Average temperature** 14°C / 57°F.

COLORADO
PLATEAU

North America USA
COLORADO PLATEAU

WHY GO *The Colorado Plateau is pleasantly warm in late May, perfect for hiking and long drives. The parks are at their greenest and the summer crowds are yet to arrive.*

Quite simply, the Colorado Plateau is home to some of the most jaw-dropping examples of landscapes to be found anywhere in the world. Dream-like spires of rock and delicate wind-carved arches stand in silence above stunning desert tableaux, while ancient rivers run through mile-deep canyons whose towering red rock walls hold a record of the past 50 million years or so. Some landscapes, such as the buttes and mesas of Monument Valley, have appeared in countless films, making them instantly recognizable. Others, like Zion's river-carved canyon, are startlingly new and fresh. Even the Grand Canyon offers refreshing vistas when viewed from the North Rim. Over 305 m (1,000 ft) higher than the more famous and desert-like South Rim, the North Rim is blanketed in cool green forest, and from the canyon edge, the Colorado

River appears as an almost-hidden glimmer thousands of feet below.

The region's spectacular wilderness is inevitably perfect for exploring on foot. Discover hidden desert sanctuaries, where translucent green pools are fed by misty waterfalls, and weirdly wonderful landscapes of red stone towers, sculpted by the wind. On the Rim Trail, wander for mile upon mile along the edge of the truly epic Grand Canyon.

One of the very best ways to travel around the region is in a motor home, which offers unparalleled freedom to explore at your own pace. There is nothing like enjoying a coffee in the early morning crispness of the desert air and anticipating the day's adventure ahead.

When Else to Go
September–October Temperatures drop after the heat of summer.

PLANNING YOUR TRIP Getting there Fly into Las Vegas airport, well served by international and domestic airlines, then drive. **Getting around** Travel by motor home or car. **Weather** Sunny, warm days and cool evenings. **Average temperature** 22°C / 72°F.

HIKES AROUND THE PLATEAU

1 **Bighorn Canyon**, found in the Grand Staircase-Escalante National Monument, is one of the easier hikes, at 12.5 km (7.8 miles).

2 **Phipps Wash** is a lovely 13.8-km (8.6-miles) hike in the Grand Staircase-Escalante National Monument. There is a small amount of scrabbling, but it's worth it for the great views atop Maverick Bridge.

3 **Salt Creek**, in the Needles District of Canyonlands National Park, has cliff dwellings and petroglyphs – reminders of the region's Ancestral Puebloan culture. At 39 km (24 miles), it's a longer hike and you'll need to look into backcountry camping.

4 **Professor Creek**, a short distance from Moab, is a really refreshing hike, as it involves paddling in shallow streams and concludes at a double-tongued waterfall. It lasts for 13 km (8 miles).

5 **The Rim Trail**, which stretches for some 21 km (13 miles) around Grand Canyon National Park, is straight-forward with fabulous vistas *(below)*.

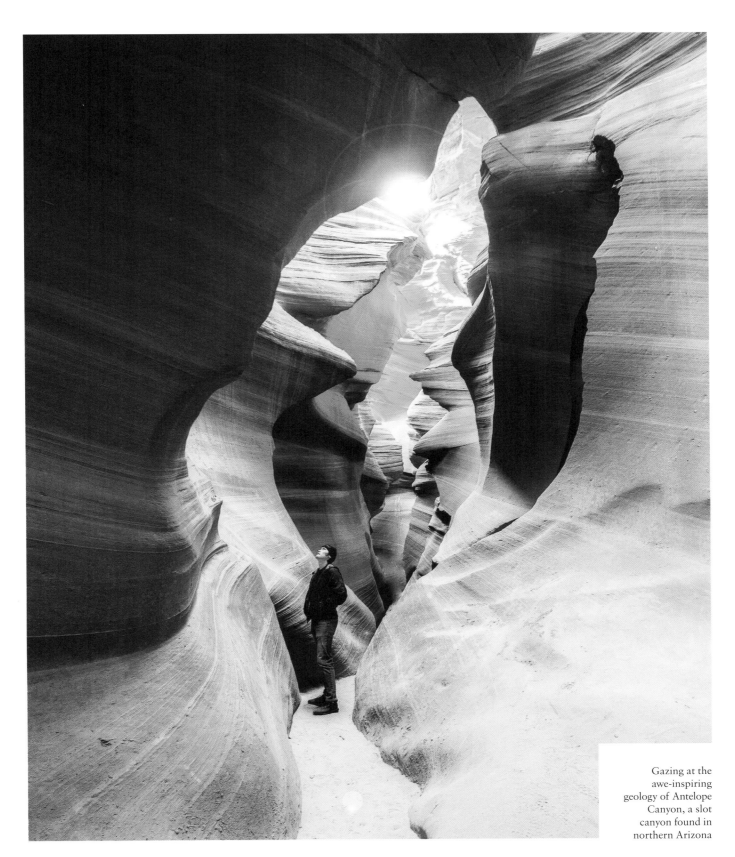

Gazing at the awe-inspiring geology of Antelope Canyon, a slot canyon found in northern Arizona

CRETE

Europe Greece
CRETE

WHY GO *Crete's summer begins with warm May days when the lowlands are draped with colourful wildflowers.*

Crucible of ancient civilizations, Crete is packed with archaeological treasures, yet it is the natural landscape that shines at this time of year. The island is wonderfully alive, with dark green olive trees, fragrant orange groves and pink oleander growing wild.

There's good walking here, most famously the Samaria Gorge, a demanding hike to the south coast and one of the most striking areas of natural beauty in Greece. Easier is the Therisso Gorge, threaded by a tiny road and edged by wildflowers. From high on the hills you are almost transported to the distant past.

When Else to Go
March Experience the exuberant carnival celebrations in Rethymno and Irakleio.

PLANNING YOUR TRIP **Getting there** Crete is an island south of Athens, with three airports: Irakleio, Chania and Sita. **Getting around** Travel by bus, taxi or hire car. **Weather** Warm and sunny. **Average temperature** 25°C / 77°F.

The small village of Sfakia, fringed by hills, on the island's south coast

Asia China
SILK ROAD

WHY GO *A journey along the Silk Road continues to capture the imagination of travellers. Make your trip in May to avoid the extreme heat of summer.*

Few routes compare to the epic Silk Road. Traversing some 7,000 km (4,300 miles), this ancient trading route was not a single highway, but a network of routes converging and diverging across Asia. Xi'an was the beginning of the north route, and it still makes a good starting point for a memorable journey of your own. Each leg of the route is a matter of minutes by plane but taking the train is recommended if you have the time – the sense of journey is much better captured watching the changing landscape and architecture through a carriage window.

The Silk Road has countless highlights. In Xi'an, see the majestic Big Wild Goose Pagoda and visit the extraordinary site of the Terracotta Army; witness Jiayuguan's imposing fort, a magnificent piece of architectural drama; and stop in Dunhuang to explore the Mogao Caves, the richest collection of Buddhist art in China. Out of your train window, gaze at decorative mosques, dusty desert and mountain scenery. This trip is raucous, dusty, hot, unmissable – but what more could you want?

When Else to Go
September–October After the heat of summer, the temperature drops and autumnal colours come into play. Avoid the blazing hot summers and bitterly cold winters.

PLANNING YOUR TRIP Getting there Xi'an is served by an international airport, though many visitors arrive via Beijing. **Getting around** The most rewarding way to see the region is by train. **Weather** Mild and springlike. **Average temperature** 23°C / 74°F.

Clockwise from top left
A mural in the Mogao Caves; the mountainous landscape of Xinjiang; Jiayuguan's elaborate fort; the terracotta warriors in Xi'an; Crescent Lake, an oasis near Dunhuang; a man selling carpets at a local bazaar

A city of contrasts: the streets of New York's Lower Manhattan and the sleek skyscrapers towering beyond

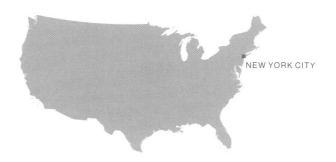

NEW YORK CITY

North America USA
NEW YORK CITY

WHY GO *One of the world's most exciting cities, New York is full of cultural riches – art, theatre, museums – alongside world-class food and shopping. Late spring is a great time to visit, with mild days and a few festivals, including the Tribeca Film Festival.*

The pulse and the pace are daunting at first, but the relentlessly fast rhythm of city life can't be ignored. Before you know it, you're dashing around like a local, eating on the run and sharing in the excitement. New York can be anything you want it to be: stylishly chic or cutting-edge trendy; a high temple of culture or a hive of commercialism.

Exploring is an unending pleasure because every neighbourhood offers a different mood and architecture, from the dazzle of Broadway neon and the cast-iron landmarks of SoHo to the glittering skyscrapers of the financial district. The best way to see it all is on foot. Stroll the Upper East Side for Beaux-Arts mansions and dozens of museums, including the Frick Collection, Frank Lloyd Wright's landmark Guggenheim and the Jewish Museum. Head to the Upper West Side for classic Art Deco apartments and even more museums.

To really feel the flavour of the city, share some other favourite pleasures with New Yorkers. Watch street performers and the passing parade of city folk from the steps of the Metropolitan Museum of Art on weekend afternoons. Browse the stalls of the farmers' Greenmarket in Union Square. Walk the East River Promenade from Brookfield Place through Battery Park, with the Statue of Liberty in view all the way. Take in a show or check out Sunday's GreenFlea market at Columbus Avenue and 77th Street. You'll quickly understand why so many love calling the Big Apple home.

When Else to Go
June Join the party during Pride and at the Puerto Rican Day Parade.
December Christmas celebrations kick off with lights and decorations aplenty.

PLANNING YOUR TRIP **Getting there** New York is served by three airports: La Guardia (domestic), JFK and Newark. **Getting around** New York is a great city to tour on foot. The subway system is comprehensive. **Weather** May is usually sunny, though there can be cold spells, so pack plenty of layers. **Average temperature** 20°C / 72°F.

// JUNE

BARCELONA, SPAIN   118

YUNNAN, CHINA   120   COAST TO COAST, CANADA   128

MONTREAL, CANADA   122   MACHU PICCHU, PERU   130

TENNESSEE, USA   123   ROME, ITALY   132

ULURU, AUSTRALIA   124   DALMATIAN COAST, CROATIA   134

ICELAND   126   KRUGER NATIONAL PARK,
                                            SOUTH AFRICA   136

The dramatic volcanic
landscape near Askja
caldera, Iceland

Above Gridded streets surrounding the unfinished Sagrada Família, designed by Antoni Gaudí

Right A firestarter performing for the Night of Fire; partygoers enjoying a performance at Sónar music festival

BARCELONA

Europe Spain
BARCELONA

WHY GO *As well as offering Barcelona's best weather, June has a cultural calendar chockfull of festivals and events. The highlight is the huge all-night celebration Sant Joan, when partygoers flock to the beach in their droves.*

Nestled between the Mediterranean and the two mountains of Montjuïc and Tibidabo, Barcelona is a naturally theatrical city. Along La Rambla – a spectacular mile-long promenade that connects the city to the sea – everyone is part of the performance, and tourists join the human statues, dancers and other entertainers who form the resident cast. Winding streets lead off into the Barri Gòtic, the city's medieval core, with its columned churches, shaded doorways, elaborate gargoyles and tiny alleys that suddenly open up onto romantic squares and sun-struck courtyards. In the Born district, medieval palaces now house art museums and lively tapas and cava bars, while cutting-edge design shops

and chic modern restaurants stand alongside the city's coolest clubs.

Mid-June sees the Sónar music festival, a three-day celebration of electronic sound and digital art and innovation. However, the real highlight of the month is Sant Joan, the "Night of Fire", on 23 June, when Barcelona is framed by giant firework displays on the surrounding hillsides. Revellers gather on the beach to dance the night away around huge bonfires, before greeting the new dawn with a bracing swim.

When Else to Go
September As the summer draws to a close, enjoy parades and parties at the Fiesta de la Mercè.

PLANNING YOUR TRIP **Getting there** The internatio nal airport, El Prat, is connected to the city centre by bus, train and taxi. **Getting around** The city is easily explored on foot and there are excellent bus and metro connections. **Weather** Reliably sunny; rain is unusual. **Average temperature** 25°C / 77°F.

Avant-garde and achingly cool, Barcelona has something for every hour of the day.

1 **Gaudí architecture** is wonderfully whimsical. Pay homage to the genius at Casa Batllo, Park Güell and – of course – the Sagrada Família.

2 **La Rambla** is the beating heart of the city, a thrumming thoroughfare where locals come to eat, drink and catch up with friends.

3 **Barcelona's nightlife** is second to none. Neighbourhoods like El Raval, El Born and Eixample are chock-full of bars and clubs.

4 **Museums** cover everything from modern art and design to the history of the city. Culture vultures won't know where to begin.

5 **Montjuïc** rises over the city with its fortress, gardens and Olympic Park. Buy a bottle of cava, catch the cable car to the top and enjoy the view.

TOP TIP

You'll find the perfect photo spot at Carrer de l'Allada-Vermell 12, in El Born. Potted plants and leafy shrubs line this gorgeously weathered apartment.

YUNNAN

Asia China
YUNNAN

WHY GO *In June, Yunnan's Tiger Leaping Gorge is swollen with rainfall, making it the perfect time to embark on a dramatic gorge walk.*

Tiger Leaping Gorge is one of China's great natural wonders. Here the Jinsha-Jiang, the River of Golden Sand, slices its way through two 5,000-m- (16,400-ft-) high peaks, Jade Dragon Snow Mountain and Haba Snow Mountain. As you hike along the narrow ridge that traces the mountainside, far below the river rages, while high above, the cloud-draped mountain soars. Each turn reveals another sublime view – it's no wonder that those completing this 32-km (20-mile) gorge trek complain of tired necks as well as knees.

When Else to Go
April Spring sees the Water Splashing Festival, which celebrates the new year in Xishuangbana.

PLANNING YOUR TRIP **Getting there** The Yunnan region is served by Kunming Changshui International Airport and intercity buses. **Getting around** Taxis are plentiful and cheap. **Weather** Mild and clear. **Average temperature** 19°C / 66°F.

The flooded Jinsha River carving its way through Tiger Leaping Gorge in a huge torrent of water

North America Canada
MONTREAL

MONTREAL

WHY GO *Montreal is a hotbed of fun in summer and the International Jazz Festival is its shining star.*

The Canadian summer is sweet and desperately short, but Montrealers are experts at making the most of it. When the snow melts, the city erupts into a seamless riot of festivals, street parties and celebrations. Any excuse will suffice: hand in a request, cordon off a sleepy *rue* and the jubilation begins. The best is the *Festival International de Jazz*, held from late June to early July. Conceived as a festival for the *peuple*, it's a 10-day extravaganza of 500 concerts held at open-air venues (free), music halls and jazz clubs. Just about everyone comes, with crowds of around two million people gathering together to enjoy the music. Legendary jazz players from all over the world queue up to join in and share a stage with the local talent, making the festival one of the best parties on the planet.

Montreal is like a jazz piece itself – it will surprise you at every turn. This dynamic city tries to be most things to most people – with culture, nightlife and shopping galore – and, with Gallic flair, it always succeeds.

When Else to Go
February Check out La Poutine Week, an extravaganza of chips, cheese curds and gravy.

PLANNING YOUR TRIP **Getting there** Trudeau International Airport is a half-hour taxi ride from the city centre. **Getting around** The metro and bus network are the most efficient ways to get around. **Weather** Showers are frequent but pass quickly. **Average temperature** 20°C / 68°F.

A jazz band performing on the main stage during the *Festival International de Jazz*

Numerous kitsch signs for honky-tonk bars along Broadway's bustling sidewalk in down-town Nashville

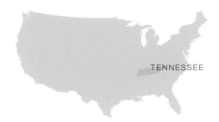

North America USA
TENNESSEE

WHY GO *For four magical days in June, hundreds of the best country music stars descend on Nashville, while Memphis rocks to the beat.*

Music, music and more music! Where else in the world can you find two cities renowned for their musical styles just a half day's drive from each other? Nashville is the home of country, and every June the city hosts the star-studded Country Music Association (CMA) Festival. For four days the city is one big party, so jump into the concert crowds, throw your hands up high, dance to the music and lip-sync the words to your favourite songs.

If Nashville is the polished centre of country, Memphis is the down-home town that cooked up rhythm-and-blues and rock'n'roll. Sun Records – where Johnny Cash and a kid named Elvis got their start – is R&B's fountainhead, but Graceland is its heart. Spend a night hitting the bars of Beale Street where you'll dig into steaming plates of gumbo, drink ice-cold beer and dance to some of the best blues in America.

When Else to Go
May The Beale Street Music Festival and the Blues Music Awards get Memphis pumping.

PLANNING YOUR TRIP **Getting there** Nashville and Memphis both have international airports, but Memphis offers more flights. **Getting around** Car hire is available at the airports. The drive between the two cities takes four hours. **Weather** Warm and humid. **Average temperature** 32°C / 90°F.

Oceania Australia
ULURU

WHY GO *This mystical red rock speaks to the soul. Visit in June, when the temperature is at its most forgiving, and try to catch the full moon rising up from behind Uluru at sunset.*

Approaching the enormous monolith of Uluru, you cannot help but be awestruck by the spectacle of this terracotta giant – the oldest temple in the world – looming over the endless desert landscape. Don't let the word "desert" fool you; the Uluru-Kata Tjuta National Park teems with wildlife and flora. Desert she-oak trees dot the landscape and birds of crimson and gold dance beneath them, feasting on flowering plants. At night, the howl of a dingo echoes eerily across the red sand.

As you tackle the four-hour trail around Uluru's circumference, you'll be constantly surprised by water holes and ancient rock art. Time your walk to end just before sunset, then settle at one of the viewing spots to see the incredible colours that peel away from the rock as the sun drops behind it.

With a 4WD vehicle, the horizon of this vast wilderness is limitless.

Marvel at the high walls of Ormiston Gorge as you walk along the riverbed. Float on your back in the Ellery Creek water hole, gazing at the ochre cliffs above. Camp among ghost gums by the Finke River, towered over by the elegant palms of Palm Valley. And don't miss Kata Tjuta – an other-worldly group of 36 domes, with gorges and valleys so hauntingly quiet that they evoke the huge spiritual significance of this strange landscape.

A few days in the red centre will change your concept of time forever. Forget your watch, for it's impossible to measure the aeons of creation evident in this ancient land.

When Else to Go

September–October Spring is a great time to visit Uluru, with comfortable temperatures and (relatively) little rain making for perfect walking and cycling conditions.

Above Uluru, set against a pink-hued sky, at dawn

Right Colourful designs on didgeridoos; pink mulla mulla flowering in the desert; ancient Aboriginal rock painting showing a hunter and a kangaroo

PLANNING YOUR TRIP **Getting there** There are daily domestic flights to Alice Springs and Ayers Rock Airport, and from nearby Yulara you can take the shuttle to Uluru. **Getting around** Hire a car in Alice Springs to explore the area. **Weather** Pleasant during the day, but temperatures at night can drop to 5°C / 42°F. **Average temperature** 19°C / 66°F.

ICELAND

Europe
ICELAND

WHY GO *With round-the-clock daylight, there's plenty of opportunity to experience all that this country has to offer, from its eponymous ice to its natural heat.*

Nearly everything ever written about Iceland refers to it as "the land of fire and ice", and for good reason – although it is a rather tired old moniker, these natural forces represent some of the island's greatest assets. Iceland literally lives and breathes geology, from sheep pastures nurtured by the rich, volcanic soil and sparkling glacial run-off, to the distinctly aromatic geothermal heat and energy that powers the country. Its expansive glaciers, active volcanoes, hot springs, geysers, lonely mountains, wild rivers and innumerable waterfalls will awe every traveller.

From May to July, the island is bathed in round-the-clock sub-Arctic daylight (notwithstanding a good measure of North Atlantic rain). You may find Iceland's prices rather high, but you can take solace in the fact that for the money, you'll be getting two days in one. As the children of the Vikings discovered long ago, that's twice the time to indulge in Iceland's decadent offerings. Trot across the moors on a horse, walk on a lonely white icefield, soothe your skin in the mineral-rich waters of the Blue Lagoon, or defeat the cold, drenching rain with an open-air soak in a hot tub. And by the time you've headed back into Reykjavík, it'll still be light enough for plenty of eating, drinking and merriment. Or, if you're tough enough, the Reykjavík *rúntur* – an all-night pub crawl under the midnight sun.

When Else to Go
September–October Before the brutal cold of midwinter arrives (though it'll still be very chilly), this is the peak time for spotting the dazzling Northern Lights.

PLANNING YOUR TRIP **Getting there** Flights arrive into Keflavík International Airport, 50 km (30 miles) west of Reykjavík. **Getting around** Hire a car or use the public bus system. For sights further afield, use bus tours. **Weather** Predominantly wet, with some rain-free days. **Average temperature** 9°C / 48°F.

Striking Mount Kirkjufell, and the Kirkjufellsfoss waterfalls, near the town of Grundarfjörður

North America Canada
COAST TO COAST

WHY GO *Summer arrives in June, bringing with it longer days, warmer temperatures and a greater chance of glimpsing Canada's famous wildlife – perfect for this spectacular journey.*

The twin ribbons of steel that stretch for thousands of kilometres across Canada have tales to tell of the travellers who have made history on this journey – mounties and military men, pioneers and poets. Built in the 1880s, these rails united a nation, weaving together the threads of a landscape as varied as the people. It's still an epic route today, following the mighty St Lawrence River to the granite outcroppings of the Canadian Shield, across the great prairie plains and through pine and spruce trees in the Rockies, and emerging from rainforests to greet the Pacific Ocean.

Ride the rails from sea to sea and you'll glimpse the old stories, set against the rhythmic sway of the train.

In the Rockies, among the saw-toothed peaks and dramatic mountains, tales tell of the explorers who found the first routes through treacherous mountain passes and the thousands of workers who built high, heart-in-mouth bridges and long tunnels into unforgiving rock.

Many travellers choose a small portion of the cross-Canada route, but the intrepid can cross the entire nation by rail between Halifax and Vancouver. So settle back in your seat, relax and let the scenes unfold outside your window. This trip is all about the journey.

When Else to Go
October As autumn arrives, forests are awash with fiery reds and oranges.

PLANNING YOUR TRIP **Getting there** Flights arrive into all major cities, including Halifax (at Stanfield International Airport). **Getting around** You can travel either east- or westbound by train, starting in Halifax or Vancouver. **Weather** Mild and humid, with cool evenings. **Average temperature** 20°C / 68°F.

WILDLIFE ENCOUNTERS

Few things can match the excitement of seeing Canada's awesome animals in the wild. Here are a few highlights.

1 Bears Grizzly, black and brown bears are found in the Rockies' national parks and remote areas, although sightings are rare.

2 Bald eagles From the train window, keep an eye out for the distinctive white head and white tail of a bald eagle, Canada's largest bird of prey.

3 Moose Canada has about one million of these solitary creatures, with their massive muzzles and broad antlers, so you're likely to see at least one.

4 Osprey This huge bird of prey lives all over Canada. Their massive nests can be seen perched on top of dead trees or hydro poles.

5 Whales Canada's coastal waters are home to various species of whale. These gentle giants are often close enough to shore to be seen from land.

"Settle back in your seat, relax and let the scenes unfold outside your window. This trip is all about the journey."

TOP TIP

Vancouver Island offers some of the best opportunities to see whales. From March to August daily whale-watching trips depart from Tofino, Ucluelet and Bamfield. The huge humpback whale is the easiest to spot.

Clockwise from top Passing through Banff National Park in the Rockies; admiring the incredible scenery through a train carriage's window; the sun setting over Peggy's Cove lighthouse in Nova Scotia, near Halifax

MACHU PICCHU

South America Peru
MACHU PICCHU

WHY GO *With clear skies and fine weather for hiking, June is when the true magic of the Salkantay trek unfolds. This route is also a great alternative to the oversubscribed Inca Trail.*

As you tread the stony trail, the glacier-saddled peak of Nevado Salkantay rears into the cobalt-blue sky. One of the most venerated by the Inca Empire, it now forms the backdrop for the region's most compelling trek, the eponymous Salkantay. Although reaching Machu Picchu is the route's main aim, the 72-km (45-mile) trail is as much about the journey as reaching the final destination.

Trekking through snow-dusted Andean landscapes, you traverse 15 different ecosystems. Purple lupins line the path, while cyan lakes are encircled by glaciated peaks. At the trek's highest point, the Salkantay Pass, you'll see the *apachetas*, small piles of stone made as offerings to the mountain spirits. At lower altitudes, the humid cloud forest guards vivid orchids and flitting hummingbirds. Keep your eyes peeled for the playful cock-of-the-rock, with its vibrant orange plumage.

Dawn on the final day breaks with the mist rolling off the mountains to reveal a stone city of exquisite agricultural terraces and ceremonial temples – welcome to Machu Picchu. Saddled between two mountain peaks in the subtropical Andean foothills, this fortress was intended to be appreciated as just one part of its spectacular natural setting. Take the perilous ascent up Huayna Picchu, the peak directly behind the city, where dizzying views of the entire complex and the serrated mountains beyond are an apt conclusion to your adventure.

When Else to Go
April and September The shoulder months promise fewer tourists and lusher scenery, with occasional rain showers triggering a bloom of vibrant wildflowers.

PLANNING YOUR TRIP **Getting there** Fly from Lima International Airport to Cusco. The Salkantay trek begins from Sallapata, 100 km (62 miles) and a three-hour drive from Cusco; transport to this point is through an organized tour or public transport. **Getting around** A five-day organized tour is the easiest way to experience the trek. **Weather** Dry and sunny, with cold nights. **Average temperature** 20°C / 68°F.

EXPERIENCE INCA PERU

The Inca Empire left behind a trail of magnificent ancient treasures throughout the Andes. Machu Picchu might be the jewel in the region's crown, but a host of lesser known remains and experiences beckon, allowing you to follow in the footsteps of the Incas.

1 Bustling **Andean markets** sell much the same vegetables as they did in Inca times.

2 Held in honor of the Sun God, **Inti Raymi** is a lively Inca festival celebrated on the winter solstice.

3 In June, a festival is held to repair the amazing **Q'eswachaka**, a rope bridge across the Río Apurimac.

4 The **Inca Jungle Trek** is a blend of thrilling activities and hiking – perfect for adventure-lovers.

5 Embark on the challenging two-day hike to **Choquequirao**, a lesser-known Inca fortress.

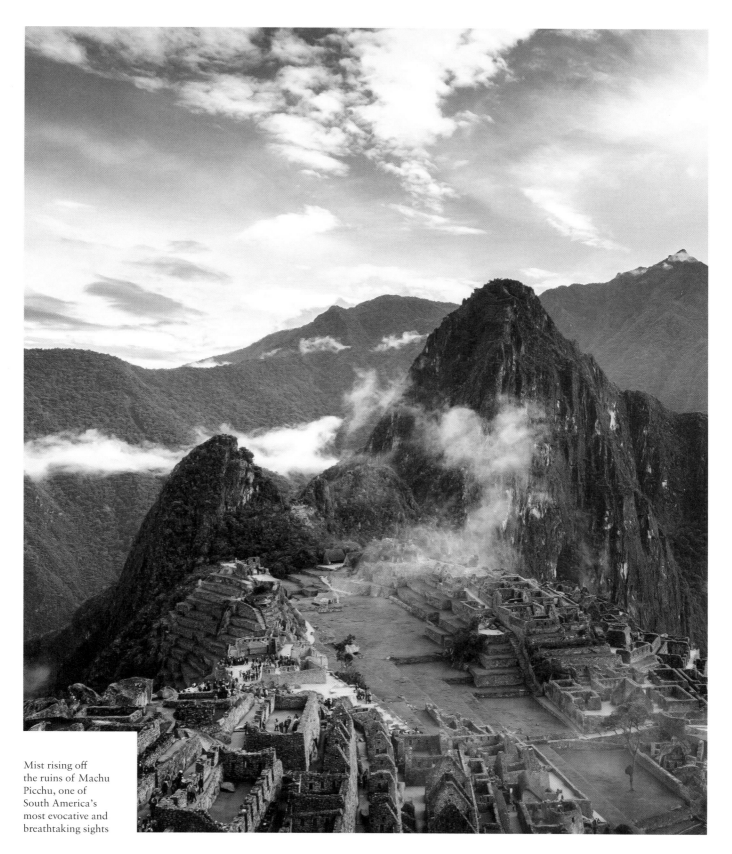

Mist rising off the ruins of Machu Picchu, one of South America's most evocative and breathtaking sights

Europe Italy
ROME

WHY GO *June is the start of the revered* Estate Romana. *During this summer festival, eclectic events are held at outdoor venues across the city, from the Imperial Forum and Villa Borghese to dozens of parks and piazzas.*

The eternal city has been attracting visitors for centuries. Some come to witness the glories of ancient Rome – the magnificent Forum, the Colosseum and the Palatine Hill. Others come to gaze up at the beautiful ceiling of the Vatican's Sistine Chapel; to browse covetously in the designer shops on the Via dei Condotti or simply to feast on the local cuisine – thin and crispy wood-fired pizzas, any of a hundred delicious pasta dishes or lightly fried courgette flowers – the ultimate taste of summer. And to finish, some homemade *gelato*.

Whatever the reason for your visit, you can't walk far without stumbling upon something extraordinary, whether it's the *Area Sacra*, where the remains of ancient temples and the rumoured site of Caesar's assassination sit in the middle of a noisy square, or Bernini's flamboyant sculptures cavorting in the fountains of the Piazza Navona. Rome has been called a living museum, but it is also very much a living city. Strolling through the old Jewish quarter or around the Campo de' Fiori, peeking into the artisans' workshops that line neighbourhood streets or exploring the alleys of the bohemian Trastevere district give a delightful insight into Roman life.

When Else to Go
April Spring in the Italian capital sees mild temperatures, fewer visitors than in the summer and all manner of Easter festivities.

PLANNING YOUR TRIP **Getting there** Rome has two airports: Leonardo da Vinci (Fiumicino) is connected to the city by train, Ciampino by bus. **Getting around** Rome is easily navigable on foot or by metro, bus and tram. **Weather** Little chance of rain. **Average temperature** 28°C / 82°F.

Right Rome's St Angel bridge at sunset

Below The Roman Colosseum, the largest amphitheatre ever built

"Some come to witness the glories of ancient Rome – the magnificent Forum, the Colosseum and the Palatine Hill."

DALMATIAN
COAST

Europe Croatia
DALMATIAN COAST

WHY GO *Calm waters and a warm climate make this a perfect time to explore the gorgeous Dalmatian Coast. And what better way to experience the seascape than to hop from one idyllic island to another?*

The Dalmatian Coast has a treasure trove of delights – a glorious combination of historic towns, Roman ruins, Venetian palaces, miles and miles of coastline washed by crystal-clear waters, and a warm, dry climate. And did we mention the islands? These are Croatia's jewels: the emerald, cypress-clad isles are set in an aquamarine sea and exquisitely finished with red-roofed towns. Follow the course of ancient explorers and negotiate the Adriatic Sea for yourself; there are a number of ferries between islands and the mainland, and private boats are available to hire.

As you hop from island to island – from Hvar to Split to Vis – you'll discover many spectacular spots to swim. The beaches are all pebbled, and those nearest to towns may be busy, but a little more effort will see you rewarded with somewhere splendidly isolated. You'll find aromatic cypress and pine forests separated from the sea by a thin border of dark rocks – uncomfortably hot to start with, they make perfect diving platforms and, afterwards, there's something wonderfully restorative about warming up on a toasty rock. If the heat gets too much, retire to the shade of the trees for a picnic lunch.

Speaking of food, there's little sustenance more satisfying than pizza and pasta. Italy may no longer lay claim to the region, but its cuisine has well and truly conquered it. And then there's Dalmatia's sumptuous seafood. What better way to experience the Dalmatian Coast than to island-hop, relaxing on each isle's beaches and gorging on its delicious cuisine?

When Else to Go

March–April Easter is a great time to visit, with locals giving brightly painted eggs as gifts. On Easter Day, eggs are hit against an opponent's; the one who emerges with an intact egg wins.

PLANNING YOUR TRIP **Getting there** The two main airports for Dalmatia are Dubrovnik Airport and Split Airport; both are about 20 km (12 miles) from their respective cities. Buses run from both airports into their city centres. **Getting around** You can hire your car at one airport and drop it off at the other. For getting around the islands there are plenty of ferries, or hire your own boat. **Weather** June is a lovely time to visit, with pleasant temperatures. This is also one of the driest months. **Average temperature** 22°C / 72°F.

Two sailing boats gliding through the calm waters near a tiny and remote island off the Dalmatian Coast

A parade of elephants
sauntering through
grassland in Kruger
National Park

KRUGER
NATIONAL PARK

Africa South Africa
KRUGER NATIONAL PARK

WHY GO *With fewer people and cooler temperatures, June is a great time for a safari in one of the world's most spectacular wildlife parks.*

Another day dawns on the plain and animals begin to stir. On the grasslands around Satara, herds of zebra breakfast on the grass, tails swishing. A pair of giraffes, stooping as though conscious of their height, move off with surprising grace. A rhino can be heard crashing around in the woods. Suddenly, a pair of pricked ears, possibly belonging to a large cat, can just be seen in the savannah grass behind the zebra... Kruger National Park has awoken.

With more varieties of animal than any other park in southern Africa, this is also one of the best places in the world to see the "Big Five". Its remarkable range of wildlife is explained by its huge variety of habitats. Amid the riverine woodland, short-sighted white rhinos lurk. North of the Olifants River, on the dry, dusty veldt, elephants amble. Along the plains south of the river, herds of zebra, giraffe and antelope sweep across the savannah. This is surely the best show on earth.

When Else to Go
February The weather is warmer, although the park does get busy with more safari expeditions.

PLANNING YOUR TRIP Getting there This park is around 500 km (310 miles) from Johannesburg, where most flights arrive into O R Tambo International Airport. Getting around The best way to travel is by car. Weather June is off-season and the weather is dry, sunny and cool (it gets cold at night). Average temperature 17°C / 63°F.

THE BIG FIVE

1 Lions are undoubtedly one of the most magnificent sights in Kruger and the park is home to one of the largest populations in Africa. You're most likely to glimpse or hear an adult lion at dawn or dusk.

2 Buffalo are the most numerous of the Big Five, and travel in herds of 10 to 20 animals. They are powerfully built and unpredictable in temperament; they can be seen fighting off predatory lions – an incredible sight.

3 Rhinos – unlike the rest of the Big Five – are solitary animals. You're likely to spot a white rhino in the southern region of Kruger, where watering halls are evenly distributed.

4 Elephants are sociable creatures and travel in matriarchal clans – males leave the herd after twelve years. They communicate by subsonic rumbling, which travels through the earth.

5 Leopards are the most elusive of the Big Five. They are nocturnal, quiet and fairly solitary. Leopards often climb trees *(below)* to escape danger and store their kills, so look up when you're exploring Kruger National Park.

// JULY

MONGOLIA 140

WASHINGTON, DC, USA 142

SALZBURG, AUSTRIA 143

PEMBROKESHIRE, WALES 144

CORSICA, FRANCE 148

BERLIN, GERMANY 150

SVALBARD, NORWAY 152

PROVENCE, FRANCE 154

COPENHAGEN, DENMARK 156

A fragrant lavender field
on a still summer's
evening, Provence

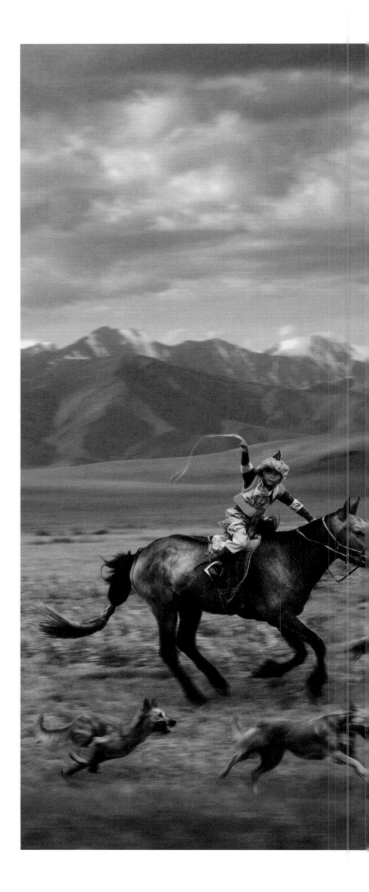

MONGOLIA

Asia
MONGOLIA

WHY GO *The traditional festival of Naadam is held throughout Mongolia every summer, with the biggest event taking place in Ulaanbaatar.*

Situated at the foot of a range of hills, Ulaanbaatar is, above all, remote. While it may have many of the trappings of a modern city, its curious mix of Soviet-inspired architecture, remnants of its pre-revolutionary history, and suburbs composed of neat rows of *gers* (traditional nomadic tents) lend it a charming air. However, getting into the countryside is the highlight of a visit to Mongolia. Most of this vast country is desert and grassland, and a major part of the population are still herdsmen of one sort or another, living as nomads.

At no time of year is this traditional lifestyle better seen than in mid-July, when the colourful Naadam Festival is held. For three days, this festival of games is celebrated. The country's greatest athletes compete in three classic Mongolian sports – horse racing, archery and wrestling. On the Mongolian steppe, horse racing is a cross-country event, which takes place over vast open grasslands and follows no set course. Dressed in Genghis Khan warrior-style costumes, the men and women who compete in these tests of stamina and strength illustrate the warrior spirit that is still intrinsic to the Mongolian character.

When Else to Go
September During shoulder season the weather is pleasantly cool.
October Bayan-Ölgii province hosts the Golden Eagle Festival.

PLANNING YOUR TRIP **Getting there** Flights arrive at Chinggis Khaan International Aiport, 18 km (11 miles) from Ulaanbaatar. **Getting around** Domestic flights and jeep transfers can be arranged. **Weather** Mongolia has short, warm summers. **Average temperature** 24°C / 75°F.

Mongolians on horseback racing across the Mongolian steppe, during the Naadam Festival

WASHINGTON, DC

WASHINGTON, DC

WHY GO *This is party time in the US capital, and the National Mall, abuzz with a whole host of music, crafts, food and entertainment, takes centre stage.*

July sees the city at its vibrant best, with two of its most important events taking place in close succession. The first, the Smithsonian Folklife Festival, celebrates cultural heritage and is an entirely free, open-air event taking place in late June or early July. During the festival, the National Mall is filled with a colourful array of musicians, artists, storytellers, cooks and craftspeople, creating an energetic celebration. This is followed with Independence Day on the Fourth of July, when a real electricity descends on the city, as fireworks explode over the Washington Monument.

Even when the excitement of these festival days has died down, there is still much to be enchanted by, from a ride on a mule-drawn barge on the Chesapeake and Ohio Canal, to the National Museum of African American History and Culture, part of the world-leading Smithsonian Institution. There is nothing stuffy about this well-ordered, historic city – beneath its austere surface you will find a very modern heart.

When Else to Go

March–April During the National Cherry Blossom Festival, the city celebrates the fragrant pink blooms that line the Mall.

PLANNING YOUR TRIP **Getting there** The city has three international airports: Dulles, Ronald Reagan Washington National Airport and Baltimore-Washington. **Getting around** The metro and metrobuses are quick and cheap. **Weather** Hot and humid. **Average temperature** 31°C / 88°F.

Balloons flying around the US Capitol on the Fourth of July

Salzburg's old town overlooked by the forbidding Hohensalzburg Fortress

SALZBURG

Europe Austria
SALZBURG

WHY GO *During sonorous Salzburg's summer festival, city evenings take on a truly elegant air.*

Music is everywhere in Mozart's stylish, picturesque city of spires and domes, narrow streets, graceful squares and pastel-painted façades. It rings out from carillons, fills the beautiful cathedral and drifts through cobbled squares where talented young musicians play impromptu concertos. Over 4,000 cultural events take place in the city throughout the year, but the most coveted tickets are for the five-week Salzburg Festival, when packed concert halls, palaces and churches resound to thrilling performances by some of the world's greatest performers. Images of the city and its surroundings never fail to beguile, but music remains at its soul.

When Else to Go
January The city celebrates the composer's birthday, on 27 January, with Mozart Week – a series of concerts.

PLANNING YOUR TRIP **Getting there** From W A Mozart airport, a bus goes to the railway station and Mirabellplatz. **Getting around** The city is easily negotiated on foot or by bike. **Weather** July is a warm month, with lots of sunshine and showers. **Average temperature** 27°C / 81°F.

PEMBROKESHIRE

Europe Wales
PEMBROKESHIRE

WHY GO *Once a land of warriors, southwest Wales is now for the adventurous. July is a lovely month to visit – the days are long, the land is lush, and the sea is cool and inviting.*

With its lush green valleys and windswept mountains, Wales is rich in natural beauty, but the butter-soft beaches and ragged coastline of Pembrokeshire, in southwest Wales, are scene-stealers. Here, dolphins frolic in the waves, seals sleep under craggy cliffs, and puffins spend their summer at Skomer Island – a rugged outcrop heaving with the little birds.

Framed by a 299-km- (186-mile-) long stretch of the Wales Coast Path, this is walking country. The landscape changes with every step as you traverse steep limestone cliffs, follow golden beaches and navigate glacial valleys. Hop from B&B to B&B, staying in cabins, family homes and shepherd's huts. Famously friendly, your hosts will likely drive any luggage on to your next stop so that it doesn't hinder your walk.

Want to get the adrenaline pumping? Don a helmet and lifejacket, find a guide and try your hand at coasteering. This extreme rock pooling will see you exploring caves and jumping into waves. If you'd rather leave it to the professionals, Abereiddi's Blue Lagoon has hosted many editions of the Red Bull Cliff Diving World Series. And the Irish Sea offers wave-riders everything from bodyboarding to surfing.

When you've worked up an appetite, chow down on tender local lamb in a gastropub, order the catch-of-the-day at a "chippy" or try laverbread – the "Welshman's caviar".

When Else to Go
September–November In autumn, fluffy grey seal pups lounge about in Pembrokeshire's pebbled coves.

Above Ragged coast-line near St Davids, Pembrokeshire

Right Walking along the Pembrokeshire Coast Path; resident puffins

PLANNING YOUR TRIP **Getting there** Cardiff is two hours by train from central London. Take the train, or drive, from there to the southwest coast. **Getting around** Five coastal bus services traverse the length of Pembrokeshire. **Weather** Days are usually warm, but be prepared for some rain. **Average temperature** 20°C / 68°F.

A gorgeous sunset over
Porthgain Harbour,
Pembrokeshire

CORSICA

Europe France
CORSICA

WHY GO *A summer playground, this island's astonishing landscape serves as the perfect backdrop for a huge range of exciting activities.*

A landscape shrouded in myth, Corsica is a place of mysterious beauty. This is a craggy, wild land, its interior peppered with peaks. Once believed to have been the home of giants and ogres, the fourth largest island in the Mediterranean is now a popular summer hotspot. And it's no surprise: it combines sunshine with charming small towns, lush green forests, cool clear rivers and soft white-sand beaches from which you can let the days drift past.

But Corsica isn't a stage set – it invites exploration. Take a horse ride through the green hills of the Castagniccia or along the sandy shores of the lovely east coast, or hire bicycles and find the perfect picnic spot. Many of Corsica's rivers are quite spectacular, ideal for canoeing or an exhilarating rafting expedition. The many footpaths are perfect for discovering some of the island's 2,000 species of flora.

When you've had your fill of activities and just want to laze in the sun and splash around in the sea, you are again spoilt for choice. Seek out the magnificent coves in the south, such as

The sun rising over Corsica's rugged Aiguilles de Bavella

Rondinara Bay, where fine white sand leads down to unbelievably clear water, or take a boat to virtually inaccessible Saleccia Beach in the north. This island really does pack a punch.

When Else to Go
May–June Early summer is a quieter time to visit the island, plus the weather is still bound to be lovely – if a little less hot than in July.

PLANNING YOUR TRIP **Getting there** Corsica has four airports: Ajaccio, Bastia, Calvi and Figari. **Getting around** Car hire is the easiest way to get around. **Weather** Generally hot and dry, but cooler in the mountains. **Average temperature** 30°C / 86°F.

CORSICA IN BLOOM

In May, hundreds of native wildflowers colour the island's *maquis* (scrubland) and fill the air with their sweet aroma.

Fenouil One of the strongest scents of the *maquis* comes from the bright yellow blooms of wild fennel, which is often used to flavour local dishes.

Myrtle This small tree is a symbol of love and immortality. It's dark-blue berries are used to make the famous *licòr di mortula*. It is also a staple of Corsican cuisine.

Sweet Broom In late spring and early summer, broom covers the hillsides in dramatic yellow swathes and delicate perfume.

BERLIN

Europe Germany
BERLIN

WHY GO *Berlin is awash with the colours of the rainbow flag in July as Pride events are held throughout the city, culminating in one of Europe's biggest and brightest street parties and parades.*

Berlin has been a centre of LGBT+ life in Germany since the early Weimar years. This combined with the city's reputation for wild parties means its annual Pride festival is one of the best in Europe, and July is packed with events – everything from drag nights to film screenings. The jewel in its crown is the Pride parade, held at the end of the month and often drawing 500,000 participants. It's a great opportunity to experience Berliners' creativity, exuberance and welcoming spirit, whether you're a member of the LGBT+ community or an ally.

The parade begins at Kurfürsten-damm, where trucks and buses play pounding music, each vying playfully with the next to attract a bigger crowd.

And what a crowd – in an event focused on inclusivity and acceptance, it's no surprise that the participants are a varied bunch. From jeans and t-shirts to full drag and rainbow bodysuits, every style of clothing is welcome. At noon the parade starts, dancing its way down the city's broad avenues and past historic buildings, finally reaching the Brandenburg Gate where there's a rousing rally.

Once the official event is over, it's time to party in clubs and bars across the city. By the time you're weaving your way home the parade route will have been cleaned up, but the remaining specks of glitter left between the cobblestones will serve as a reminder that the city's Weimar-era dreams are alive and well.

When Else to Go
May The bitter cold of winter has dissipated and open-air events across the city begin in earnest.

PLANNING YOUR TRIP **Getting there** Flights arrive into Tegel Airport, 12 km (7 miles) northwest of Berlin, and Schönefeld, 18 km (11 miles) southeast of the city. Both are easily accessible by public transport. Berlin Brandenburg is also under construction; the opening is scheduled for 2020, after which Tegel may close. **Getting around** The public transport system is made up of the U-Bahn and S-Bahn, buses and trams. **Weather** Warm and sunny, with occasional showers. **Average temperature** 23°C / 73°F.

Clockwise from top *My God, Help Me to Survive This Deadly Love* by Dmitri Vrubel, a mural on the Berlin Wall; a rainbow flag waving in front of the landmark Berlin TV Tower; a Pride participant wearing elaborate make-up

Europe Norway
SVALBARD

WHY GO *Norway's glacial outpost enjoys the 24-hour sunshine of the Arctic summer. The archipelago is home to stunning wildlife, including polar bears, which you're most likely to see in July.*

Bathed in the perpetual sunlight of midsummer, Svalbard in July presents an unrivalled glimpse of the polar north. After most of the pack ice has retreated and snow has melted in low-lying areas, boats arrive in their dozens, migrating birds return to nest on towering sea cliffs and wildflowers emerge to splash colour across the lonely, treeless tundra of this Arctic archipelago.

The Svalbard experience begins in the town of Longyearbyen, which nestles near the foot of two glaciers at the mouth of Adventdalen Valley. Perhaps because the sun is visible around the clock from mid-April to October, the tempo of life is upbeat in the summer, with locals partying into the early hours. Just outside of town, however, the wilderness begins, inspiring a real sense of adventure and discovery. The biting wind carries the cries of sea birds – puffins, guillemots, cormorants, gulls and others – that occupy cliff-hugging nests, rearing the season's chicks. Along tame shorelines, it's a joy to wander over the landscape in search of wild-flowers and the rusting remnants of adventurers past. There's a chance of spotting a reindeer or a wandering Arctic fox, but surely no wildlife experience compares with the thrill of seeing a polar bear lumbering across the icy tundra and, given that there are more polar bears than people here, it is not such an unlikely sight.

When Else to Go
September The last chance to see polar bears before the archipelago freezes over.

PLANNING YOUR TRIP
Getting there Svalbard Airport is in Longyearbyen, with flights arriving from Tromsø, 1,000 km (600 miles) south. **Getting around** An organized tour or cruise is recommended, or you can hire a car. **Weather** July is mostly dry but cold, with bracing winds. **Average temperature** 5°C / 41°F.

"Just outside of town, however, the wilderness begins, inspiring a real sense of adventure and discovery."

Clockwise from top left
A polar bear and her cubs crossing pack ice in Spitsbergen, north-west of Longyearbyen; summer meltwater forming a waterfall on an ice cap in Svalbard; a lone reindeer standing on grassland

PROVENCE

Europe France
PROVENCE

WHY GO *During the height of summer, the landscape is peppered with fields of purple lavender and the air is heavy with its sweet perfume.*

Vast sunflower prairies and violet-hued lavender fields are illuminated in the summer sun, their regimented rows fading to a distant horizon. This is quintessential Provence. July may be the busiest month to visit this most dazzling corner of France, but it is also the most magical. Throughout the summer, whole hillsides are awash with glorious shades of deep purple, plum and blue-violet. For the classic view head to the Abbaye Notre-Dame de Sénanque, where blossoms create a bee-buzzing haze of colour, scent and sound around the ancient cloisters. The Valensole Plateau is another favourite, where numerous sunflower and lavender fields are easily reachable by car.

When Else to Go
September As summer crowds start to dwindle the grape harvest season begins.

PLANNING YOUR TRIP **Getting there** The main airports are Marseille Provence and Nice Côte d'Azur. **Getting around** The coast is served by reliable bus and train networks. **Weather** Hot and dry. **Average temperature** 24°C / 75°F.

Seemingly endless rows of purple lavender in full bloom on the Valensole Plateau

Right Enjoying a ride at Tivoli on a summer's evening

Below Bikes and barges lining Nyhavn, Copenhagen's most iconic canal

COPENHAGEN

Europe Denmark
COPENHAGEN

WHY GO *Famously cool Copenhagen is abuzz in July, with locals flocking to the pretty canals and sprawling parks that pepper the Danish capital. There are plenty of summer events to keep you entertained, including a number of music festivals.*

Throngs of cyclists expertly navigate the city's streets and bridges, pausing to chat and enjoy a cup of coffee. The city's numerous parks are sprinkled with Copenhageners enjoying picnics, walking their dogs, playing frisbee and generally indulging in the Danish art of *hygge*. Photogenic waterways lined with veteran barges thrum with locals and visitors rubbing shoulders as they eat, drink and put the world to rights, and – in the designated swimming zones – the sounds of splashing and infectious laughter ring out. Welcome to wonderful Copenhagen.

A city break in Copenhagen wouldn't be complete without a visit to Tivoli, an amusement park with more rides than you can fit into a day – from simple carousels to twisting roller coasters, plus concerts, restaurants and beautiful gardens that are bursting with blooms in July. At dusk, a hundred thousand soft-glow lights turn Tivoli into an enchanting fairyland.

This utterly magical city, with its medieval cobbled streets and trendy neighbourhoods, also welcomes a plethora of music festivals in July. With the Copenhagen Opera Festival, Roskilde Festival and Copenhagen Jazz Festival, music fills the streets until the late hours. Draw up a chair, grab a drink, sit back and enjoy.

When Else to Go
October Halloween at Tivoli and autumn colours throughout the city.

PLANNING YOUR TRIP **Getting there** Copenhagen has excellent connections by air, rail, road and sea. Frequent trains shuttle from Kastrup Airport to the city centre in 15 minutes. **Getting around** There's a superb public transport system of buses, metro, waterbuses, trains and city bikes. **Weather** July is usually the sunniest month, with long and mild days. **Average temperature** 22°C / 72°F.

// AUGUST

BOROBUDUR, INDONESIA   **160**

LUCERNE, SWITZERLAND   **162**

BLACK FOREST, GERMANY   **163**

MANU NATIONAL PARK, PERU   **164**

YELLOWSTONE NATIONAL
PARK, USA   **166**

GLACIER BAY
NATIONAL PARK, USA   **168**

KANDY TO ELLA, SRI LANKA   **170**

SLOVENIA   **172**

MOZAMBIQUE, AFRICA   **174**

Steam rising from Castle
Geyser in Yellowstone
National Park

BOROBUDUR

Asia Indonesia
BOROBUDUR

WHY GO *With the rains long finished, the skies are mercifully clear, providing the perfect backdrop to this sublime monument.*

Travelling through the lush plantations and terraced rice fields of central Java, you don't see Borobudur until you arrive at the gateway to the monument. Then, through the flame trees and palm groves, it suddenly materializes.

One of the world's largest religious monuments, with nine levels, towers, niches and countless stupas, Borobudur's power lies in its five levels of sublime carvings. Be prepared for a long walk as you examine the images at the lower levels, which depict daily life in the 8th century, and, further up, dedications to the life of the Buddha. At the upper levels, the smaller stupas contain meditating Buddhas but, at the top, the central stupa is mysteriously empty, suggesting nirvana, the ultimate state of nothingness. Emerging from this, with just the sky above you and the plains stretching out below towards the awesome Merapi volcano, the most active on earth, you will suddenly feel liberated. The serenity may be short-lived – this is the country's most popular site – but, as you return through the tropical countryside, you cannot help but feel that you've had a vision of the divine.

When Else to Go
October The rainy season is yet to begin but already the surrounding countryside appears green and lush.

The majestic Borobudur, an 8th–9th-century Buddhist temple, at sunset

PLANNING YOUR TRIP **Getting there** International flights arrive at Jakarta, which is linked to Yogyakarta and Solo airports. **Getting around** Arrange a tour from Yogyakarta. **Weather** Warm and humid. **Average temperature** 27°C / 80°F.

LUCERNE

Europe Switzerland
LUCERNE

WHY GO *Coincide your visit to this enchanting medieval city with its international classical music festival.*

Surrounded by mountains on the western shore of the lake that shares its name, there can be few festival towns that enjoy Lucerne's idyllic setting. The city's reputation as a leading classical and contemporary music hub is well established and its annual festival, an impressive display of symphony concerts, galas and opera, attracts music fans in their thousands.

Should it set in, festival fatigue can easily be dispersed by a trip to the mountains. Reach the top via the world's steepest cogwheel railway and gasp at the panorama before you – flower-carpeted meadows leading down to the lakeside town, where, as dusk falls, myriad lights begin to twinkle.

When Else to Go
February/March Join the locals as they don masks and costumes for a few days of merriment and music during *fasnacht*.

PLANNING YOUR TRIP **Getting there**
Arrive into Zürich then travel by car or train.
Getting around Lucerne is best explored on foot.
Weather Warm with occasional cloudy days.
Average temperature 25°C / 77°F.

The picturesque wooden Chapel Bridge, crossing over the sheer waters of Lucerne's River Reuss

Europe Germany
BLACK FOREST

WHY GO *August is the perfect time to visit the Black Forest as the days are long, warm and sunny – great for getting out and about in the hills and mountains.*

BLACK FOREST

If you ever wanted to see the archetypal fairytale forest, visit the Schwarzwald (Black Forest). Here you'll discover dreamy country-side with rolling hills, mountainous ridges and deep river gorges; crystal-clear lakes, perfect for a cooling dip; and welcoming villages.

The area is a paradise for outdoor enthu-siasts who want a great adventure and, of course, there are hundreds of miles of well-marked hiking paths. Many follow century-old trails, forging a path through wooded valleys, past charming villages and glacier lakes. If you make it into the mountains, the Black Forest is also famous for its hot springs and healthy waters. Here you can relax in a steam sauna or simply float in a hot tub, drifting away into your own fairytale.

When Else to Go
July Hot, sultry days transform into incredible thunder storms, which make for dramatic photographs. **December** Christmas markets spring up in nearly every town in the region.

PLANNING YOUR TRIP **Getting there** Fly into Frankfurt, then travel on to Baden-Baden, near the Black Forest. **Getting around** Use Germany's excellent trains or hire a car. **Weather** Sunny and mild days. **Average temperature** 20°C / 68°F.

Morning mist settling over the Black Forest

MANU NATIONAL PARK

South America Peru
MANU NATIONAL PARK

WHY GO *Described as the most biodiverse protected area on the planet, Manu National Park is ripe for exploration. Come during the dry season to ensure access to hiking trails.*

Manu National Park is the largest tropical park in South America, and home to an extraordinary diversity of plants and wildlife. Found in this jungle are more than 850 species of bird, including the cock-of-the-rock, 200 species of mammal, such as the majestic jaguar, and more than 15,000 species of plant. All of this is remarkably preserved due to the inaccessibility of the area and monitoring of visitor numbers. No commercial activity is permitted here and tourists are not allowed to stay overnight in the park, so you'll stay in a rustic lodge (limited or no electricity and accessible only by boat), located just outside.

Hiking along forested trails in search of tapir and the elusive jaguar brings out the adventurer in visitors. On the river, the boat becomes silent as everyone waits with bated breath for the slick head of a rare giant otter to emerge from the water, or for a black cayman to catch the light as it slides into the mud. Ploughing deeper into the reserve aboard a motor-canoe, the foliage becomes thicker, the humidity more intense, and the chattering of monkeys and birds and the steady hum of insects almost deafening. The scale of the jungle is breathtaking. For sheer wilderness, it doesn't get much better than this.

When Else to Go
November Come at the start of the rainy season to see more amphibians.

PLANNING YOUR TRIP **Getting there** Fly into Lima and then on to Cusco. A further short flight on a small twin-engined plane will get you to Boca Manú. A motorized canoe takes you on the 90-minute trip down the Madre de Dios River to your accommodation. **Getting around** In the park all your trips, on land or water, will be with a guide. **Weather** The dry season can be quite humid. **Average temperature** 18–31°C / 64–88°F.

"The boat becomes silent as everyone waits with bated breath for the slick head of a rare giant otter to emerge from the water."

Above The lush green mountains of Manu

Left A kaleidoscope of macaws on a clay lick; the elusive jaguar

YELLOWSTONE
NATIONAL PARK

North America USA
YELLOWSTONE NATIONAL PARK

WHY GO *August brings the best weather, and while this is a popular time for visitors, you can avoid the bulk of the crowds if you stray from the beaten track.*

More than half a million years ago, a gargantuan volcanic explosion blanketed western North America in ash and scooped out a vast caldera 72 km by 50 km (45 miles by 30 miles) wide. Today that caldera, located just north of the spectacular Grand Teton Mountains, is green and lush with meadows and an incredible diversity of wildlife. Stunning tableaus of wild rivers, azure lakes and snow-capped peaks set the backdrop for an other-worldly landscape of steaming fumaroles, geysers, bubbling mud pots and psychedelically coloured thermal springs. This is Yellowstone National Park.

Though August is a busy time, discovering the real wilderness beauty of Yellowstone is as simple as getting off the beaten track anywhere in the park. Criss-crossing the grassy flats and mountain plateaus, pine forests and limestone terraces is a 2,000-km (1,300-mile) trail system, providing plenty of opportunity to find solitude. A walk along the South Rim Trail east from busy Artist Point leads you up a brief, steep ascent that takes you far from the crowds. Following the gentle terrain of the canyon rim, the trail offers stunning views of the canyon, the Yellowstone River and the cascading cataract of lower falls that are as visually captivating as they were when the park was first discovered.

When Else to Go

May Avoid the crowds and visit the park as it's opening up again. This is a great time for wildlife, too: look out for bison calves and bear cubs.

PLANNING YOUR TRIP **Getting there** The closest major international airport to Yellowstone National Park is in Salt Lake City, Utah; alternatively, fly into regional airports in Wyoming, Montana or Idaho. **Getting around** Hire a car in Salt Lake City for the 515-km (320-mile) drive to Yellowstone. **Weather** August days are long and warm. Thunderstorms are frequent. **Average temperature** 30°C / 86°F.

HIKES AROUND THE PARK

1 Old Faithful is the park's most famous geyser, but there are more to see. Follow the **Norris Geyser Basin Trail** through this geothermal hot spot to discover rare acid ones like Echinus Geyser.

2 See bison, grizzly bears and elk from the **Hayden Valley Trail**, between Yellowstone Lake and the Grand Canyon of Yellowstone.

3 Family-favourite **Trout Lake Loop** is great for wildlife spotting. See otters frolicking in the water during the summer months.

4 There are hikes for all levels around the rim of the Grand Canyon of the Yellowstone. The **Artist Point Trail** leads to particularly lovely views of the canyon and Lower Yellowstone Falls.

5 The strenuous **Avalanche Peak Trail** takes you to superb views of the park's tallest peaks. July and August is the sweetspot between snowfall and grizzly season.

TOP TIP

There is a wealth of information at the park's visitors' centres. Pick up park maps and brochures, get the latest updates on wildlife viewing, and peruse well-curated exhibits on Yellowstone's history, geology and wildlife.

"Stunning tableaus of wild rivers, azure lakes and snow-capped peaks set the backdrop for an otherworldly landscape."

Clockwise from top An aerial view of the Grand Prismatic Spring; the Mammoth Hot Springs; bison grazing the prairie below the Grand Teton Mountains

GLACIER BAY
NATIONAL PARK

North America USA
GLACIER BAY NATIONAL PARK

WHY GO *Whale-watching opportunities are at a high during summer, as whales return to Alaska's waters after spending the winter in warmer climes.*

Little compares to seeing a house-sized block of ice crashing into the water or a huge humpback whale seemingly defying gravity as it breaks the surface, but these scenes are common in Alaska's Glacier Bay.

In this ever-changing landscape of impressive glaciers, snowcapped mountains and icy waters, there is abundant wildlife. On a good day, you might see the spouting and splashing of breaching whales, hear the cries of sea birds, watch comical sea otters play and bald eagles wheel overhead, and perhaps even a brown bear methodically plodding along the shore. But the real thrill is in watching a massive block of ice dislodge from the glacier face and slide silently into the sea. A second or two later comes the thunderous crack of the breaking ice, followed by a line-up of swells that cause your boat to bob up and down like a cork. This is nature at its most sublime.

When Else to Go
April Combine a visit to Glacier Bay with the annual Alaska Folk Festival, held in Juneau, for a week of concerts and dances.

PLANNING YOUR TRIP Getting there Fly from Juneau International Airport to Gustavus, 16 km (10 miles) from the park headquarters at Bartlett Cove. There are also ferries but many visitors arrive by cruise ship. **Getting around** The bay is best seen aboard cruise ships, tour boats and kayaks. **Weather** Cool and often rainy, with some sunny periods. **Average temperature** 14°C / 57°F.

Kayaking on icy waters in the epic Glacier Bay National Park, surrounded by mountain scenery

KANDY

ELLA

Asia Sri Lanka
KANDY TO ELLA

WHY GO *The "Tea Train" from Kandy to Ella serves up a seductive blend of spectacular scenery and Sri Lankan sociability. The rains have eased too, so the view from your carriage is totally unspoiled.*

There are few things that withstand a "world's most beautiful" moniker, but the train journey that runs through Sri Lanka's Hill Country pulls it off. This is a region of mist-shrouded mountains, rolling hillsides carpeted with lush green tea plantations and rushing waterfalls – and there's no better way to see it than from the window of a train.

Built to transport tea from the hills to the country's capital, Colombo, the railways snaking through the region have become a hit with travellers. The route from Kandy to Ella takes around seven hours but the most memorable section is the four hours from Hatton to Ella, at the highest point of the line. As the train grinds patiently upwards, increasingly majestic views over the craggy green hills are revealed. Tea is everywhere: a seemingly endless swathe of bright green bushes creeping up impossible gradients, speckled with the tiny figures of Tamil tea-pickers hunched over the bushes. As the train winds its way through valleys there are glimpses of dozens of waterfalls cascading

down cliff faces, while from cliff edges mist and cloud transforms the landscape into a mysterious milky blur.

Regular stops at a series of quaint, toy-like stations, complete with their original hand-painted signs and colonial-era fittings, punctuate the journey. Carriages are visited by roving hawkers waving bunches of bananas and freshly fried piles of samosas, before a deafening blast of the horn signals departure time, and the train rolls slowly onwards again.

When Else to Go
April The Hill Country is alive as the locals celebrate the Sinhalese–Tamil New Year with ten days of festivities.

PLANNING YOUR TRIP **Getting there** Fly into Colombo International Airport **Getting around** From Colombo, board the train to Kandy then on to Ella. Tickets go on sale 30 days in advance; book early. **Weather** Warm with regular showers; evenings are cool. **Average temperature** 25°C / 77°F.

Right Picking tea in the Hill Country; train timetable at Kandy station

Below Enjoying the view aboard the "Tea Train" from Kandy to Ella

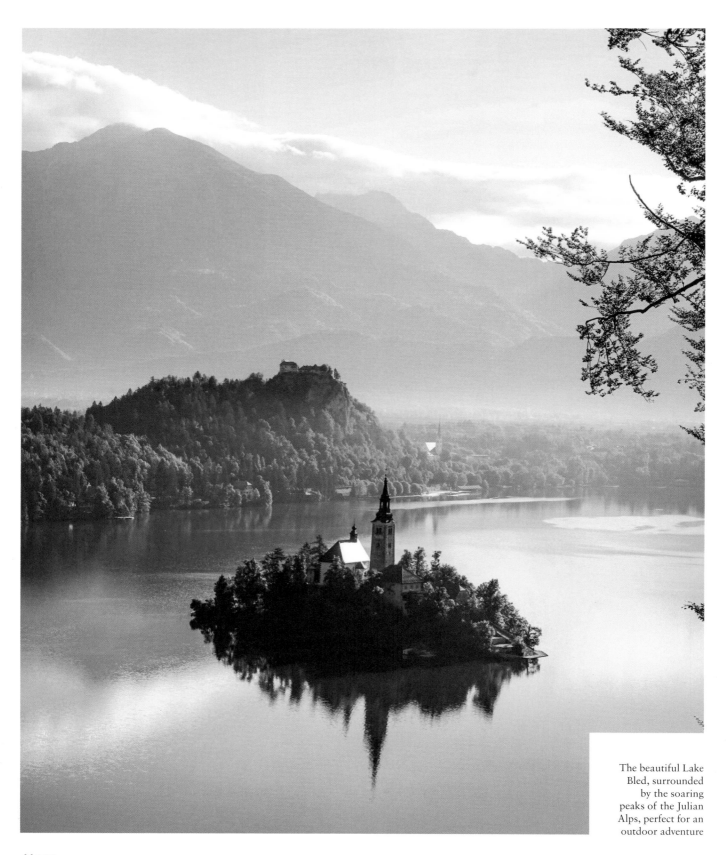

The beautiful Lake Bled, surrounded by the soaring peaks of the Julian Alps, perfect for an outdoor adventure

SLOVENIA

Europe
SLOVENIA

WHY GO *Make the most of long, warm days during Slovenia's summer and plan an active break in the country's scenic settings.*

Blessed with voluminous snow-capped mountain peaks, sparkling lakes, gushing waterfalls and glacial valleys, Slovenia is packed with picture-perfect views. One of the most iconic images of the country is the ethereal Lake Bled, lauded by local poet France Prešeren as "this second Eden, full of charm and grace". Admiring its mist-shrouded island church, which reclines under the protective eye of Bled Castle and the vaulting mountain peaks of the Julian Alps, it's hard to disagree.

The true joy in a visit to Slovenia, however, is getting out and about in its unspoiled countryside. This is truly an outdoor destination, with hiking, trekking, mountain biking, caving and canyoning all on offer. In Triglav, the country's only national park, hiking 2,864 m (9,400 ft) to the summit of the park's eponymous mountain is something of a rite of passage for Slovenes – so why not join them? In nearby Bohinj there is even more unspoiled countryside ripe for exploration and Slovenia's largest lake, the glacial Lake Bohinj. This stunning expanse of alpine water is framed by the hulking mountains, with picturesque lake cruises and a range of outdoor sports like paragliding, kayaking and horse riding available during the long summer days.

South of the Julian Alps in the Soča Valley, a water wonderland awaits, where, amid rugged mountain peaks and leafy forest, the brilliant emerald-coloured Soča River attracts whitewater rafters from all over Europe. If a white-knuckle ride on the river isn't for you then try a canoe or mountain bike trip instead. Whatever you go for, you're guaranteed a memorable alpine adventure.

When Else to Go

October Visit to see the spectacular autumn colours and make the most of the harvest season on a wine-tasting tour.

PLANNING YOUR TRIP **Getting there** International flights arrive in the capital, Ljubljana. **Getting around** An efficient bus network links most places to Ljubljana but rail services are more limited. Car hire is recommended. **Weather** Days are pleasantly warm but it can get a lot colder at higher altitudes. **Average temperature** 25°C / 77°F.

WILD SWIMMING SPOTS

Slovenia's crystal-clear lakes, glittering rivers and spectacular waterfalls make this an ideal location for a refreshing dip.

The blue-green **Lake Bled** is the most iconic of Slovenia's lakes. The designated swimming area is near the magnificent castle rock.

Just 15 km (9 miles) south of Ljubljana, **Podpeško Lake** is the locals' choice. It also happens to be the deepest lake in Slovenia.

Lake Jasna comprises two small artificial lakes. Set against a backdrop of jagged mountain peaks, the view from this alpine lake is nothing short of breathtaking.

MOZAMBIQUE

Right Snorkelling through a coral reef; a humpback whale, off the coast; three bottlenose dolphins

Below Azure waters and golden sands in the Bazaruto Archipelago

Africa
MOZAMBIQUE

WHY GO *Visit Mozambique in August to see migrating humpback whales and frolicking dolphins.*

Long one of Southern Africa's least known destinations, Mozambique is rapidly gaining a reputation as a diving mecca. Its magnificent coastline, over 2,000 km (1,240 miles) long and speckled with islands, is home to myriad marine life and little-explored coral reefs perfect for an underwater adventure.

A highlight is the Bazaruto Archipelago. Seen from above, brilliant turquoises, aquas and deep blues swirl together with green and jade tones, all in stunning contrast to the shimmering white sand banks and beaches. In the water, humpback whales and dolphins share the sea with an impressive array of beautiful tropical fish. Still a little-visited jewel on a vast continent, Mozambique's many treasures truly are spectacular.

When Else to Go
September The dry season continues providing plenty of opportunity for a beach holiday.

PLANNING YOUR TRIP **Getting there** Fly into Johannesburg, then on to Maputo, Mozambique's capital. **Getting around** From Maputo, internal flights connect to the Bazaruto Archipelago. **Weather** Sunny, dry and warm. **Average temperature** 24°C / 75°F.

// SEPTEMBER

MUNICH, GERMANY **178**

GALWAY, IRELAND **179**

NAMIB-NAUKLUFT PARK, NAMIBIA **180**

NORTHEAST VERMONT, USA **182**

LYCIAN COAST, TURKEY **184**

LONDON, ENGLAND **186**

BORNEO, INDONESIA **188**

BEIJING, CHINA **190**

QUEENSTOWN, NEW ZEALAND **192**

MADEIRA, PORTUGAL **193**

Ballooning over the
sweeping ochre dunes
of Namibia's Namib-
Naukluft Park

Europe Germany
MUNICH

WHY GO *Join the locals for Oktoberfest, the world's biggest beer festival, a boisterous yet charming celebration of German Gemütlichkeit (sociability), with beer, Brez'n (pretzels) and partying.*

MUNICH

Despite its name, Oktoberfest usually starts in September, under the autumn sun. Over the course of 16 days, Munich moves to the joyous sounds of oompah bands, clinking steins and a constant chorus of *"prost!"* (cheers). Over 6 million dirndl- and lederhosen-clad visitors descend on the city every year to drink some 60,000 hectolitres (10.5 million pints) of beer. The favourite tents enjoy such incredible hype that reservations are necessary. But what do you expect at an uber party like this?

When Else to Go
December Marienplatz, the city's central square, hosts one of Germany's prettiest Christmas markets.

PLANNING YOUR TRIP **Getting there** Munich International Airport is well connected. **Getting around** Explore the centre on foot. **Weather** Sunny and dry. **Average temperature** 16°C / 60°F.

Freshly shucked
oysters garnished
with lemons

Revellers drinking
steins of beer
in one of
Oktoberfest's
most popular tents

Europe Ireland
GALWAY

GALWAY

WHY GO *Wash oysters down with pints of the "black stuff" during this foodie festival that hits the city of Galway at the end of September.*

During the four-day Galway International Oyster and Seafood Festival, the emphasis rests on fun, food and, of course, filling up with Guinness – the national drink. The main attraction of the festivities is the oysters, which are carefully selected from beds within the pure waters of Galway Bay, where the native oyster still grows wild.

On Saturday afternoon the "cracking" Guinness World Oyster Opening Championships starts off the proceedings, with eager competitors frantically trying to beat the shucking world record. For the next three days, festival-goers can sample these succulent, salty oysters in the festival marquee, while they listen to buoyant live music or watch one of the nation's hottest chefs demonstrate how to prepare the decadent shellfish for themselves.

If oysters aren't for you, don't despair. The festival runs a programme of foodie-oriented talks on a variety of subjects and some of Galway's best restaurants host tasting events to coincide with the festival. Don't miss, too, the Mardi-Gras-style Gala Event, when the walk past the Spanish Arch to Nimmo's Pier – where the marquee is erected – takes you through a sea of high heels and *haute couture*. Whether you're drinking, dancing or devouring oysters, there is always more than enough *craic* to go round.

When Else to Go
July Ireland is at its warmest at the height of summer and the Galway International Arts Festival brings actors, musicians and artists to the city.

PLANNING YOUR TRIP Getting there Galway Airport is 10 km (6 miles) from the city centre and is accessible by internal fights from Dublin Airport. **Getting around** There are taxis and buses, but the centre is easily covered on foot. **Weather** Generally mild, but rain is not unusual. **Average temperature** 12°C / 54°F.

NAMIB-NAUKLUFT PARK

Africa Namibia
NAMIB-NAUKLUFT PARK

WHY GO *At the height of the dry season, Namibia's wildlife congregate around rare rivers and oasis-like waterholes. This makes September one of the best times to visit this lunar landscape.*

Namibia must rank close to being the emptiest non-polar nation on the planet. Dominated by the Namib Desert, whose parched sandy soils are teased by less than 2.5 cm (1 inch) of rain annually, this immense land is too desiccated to sit comfortably with adjectives such as pretty or beautiful. And yet there is a vastness to the Namibian landscape, a ravaged majesty that is at once humbling and breathtaking.

The 50,000-sq-km (19,000-sq-mile) Namib-Naukluft – one of Africa's largest national parks – is home to Sossusvlei. Here you'll find the world's tallest dunes: rippled apricot mountains whose curvaceous "scorpion tails" tower above a series of seasonal pans that fill with water once or perhaps twice in a decade. Here, too, is the aptly named Deadvlei, its embalmed floor of cracked mud hosting a spectral forest, a relic of the days when this parody of a lake received water more regularly.

Come dusk, you might see a herd of oryx antelope filing regally across a dune crest, a meerkat family standing to attention in the dying light or a spiky quiver tree silhouetted against the disappearing sun. The crisp, clear desert air and absence of competing light sources make the Namib night sky a thing of shimmering, awe-inspiring beauty. No less memorable is the silence of the desert on a windless night: so close to absolute that it becomes almost tangible, an enveloping presence broken sporadically by the gentle chatter of a gecko or the demented whooping of a distant hyena or jackal.

When Else to Go
March–April Featuring a parade, music performances and a masked ball, Windhoek Karneval (WIKA) is the premier event in Namibia's calendar. Its origins lie in the country's time as a German colony.

The skeleton of a dead tree silhouetted against the white clay pan of Deadvlei

PLANNING YOUR TRIP **Getting there** Namibia's international airport, Hosea Kutako, is 46 km (28 miles) from the capital, Windhoek. **Getting around** A car is essential, even within the National Park. To the north, the cities of Windhoek and Swakopmund are connected by roads, as well as daily flights. **Weather** Dry and pleasantly warm. Cold at night and in the morning. **Average temperature** 25°C / 77°F.

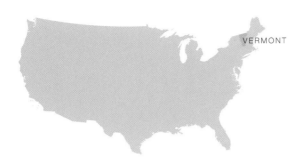

VERMONT

North America USA
NORTHEAST VERMONT

WHY GO *The flaming hues of Vermont's autumn foliage are an annual spectacle. Enjoy the colours without the crowds in the state's rugged and remote "Northeast Kingdom".*

With its bucolic mountains and rolling hills, Vermont is arguably one of the most scenic corners of America, blessed with an abundance of sugar maple trees that not only produce the Green Mountain State's famous maple syrup, but are responsible for the distinctive bright red leaves that make this one of autumn's most colourful destinations.

Leaf peepers look no further. A scenic drive through Vermont's unspoiled rural northeast, known simply as the "Kingdom" to understandably empassioned locals, will reveal Norway maples ablaze in scarlet and orange, sugar maples in cardinal red, and birches, beeches and alders aglow in luminous yellow. This is where the spectacle of the changing seasons is at its most dramatic. But Northeast Vermont offers so much more than great views from behind the wheel. Here you'll find farm stands filled to the brim with freshly harvested goodies, inviting restaurants that celebrate farm-to-fork produce, quaint country stores and charming inns, not to mention the many eclectic museums and antique stores.

A particular highlight is the annual Northeast Kingdom Foliage Festival, which rotates from town to town for a week during late September and early October. Each town hosts its own day and offers all manner of exciting activities, from guided ghost walks through the pretty town of Peacham to artisan cheese tasting in Cabot, all set against a beautiful backdrop of vibrant autumn colour.

When Else to Go
February Hit the slopes when ski season is in full swing.

Above A spectacular display of colour on the banks of Long Pond, Greensboro

Right Freshly harvested sweetcorn; walking through the woodland in Vermont; autumnal colours in Peacham

---

PLANNING YOUR TRIP Getting there Vermont's major airport is in Burlington, 124 km (77 miles) from St Johnsbury. More international flights arrive into Boston, 240 km (150 miles) away. **Getting around** Hiring a car is the best way to tour this leafy corner of New England. **Weather** Mild but changeable. **Average temperature** 18°C / 64°F.

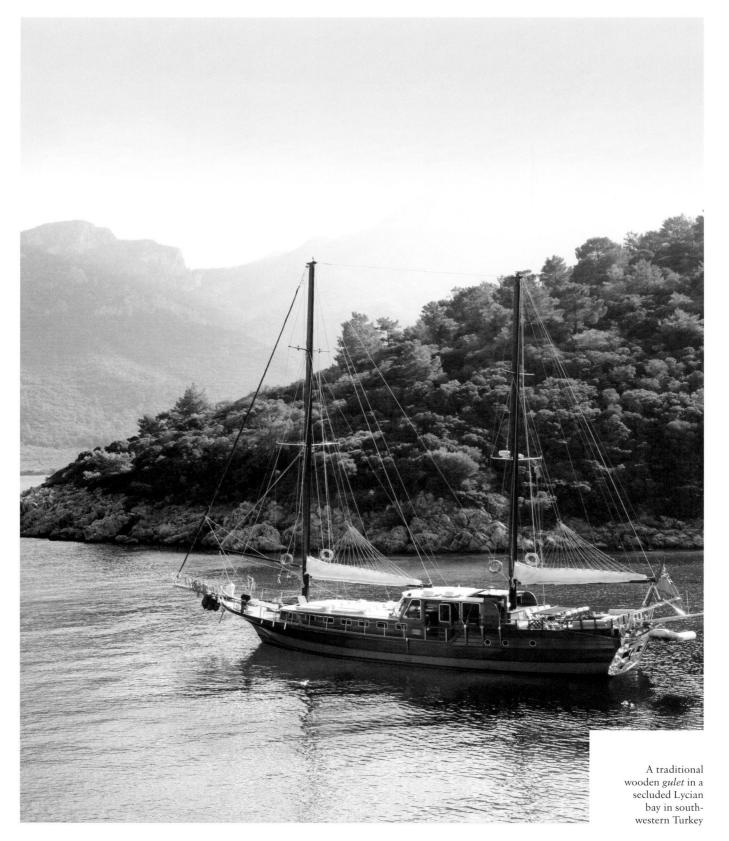

A traditional
wooden *gulet* in a
secluded Lycian
bay in south-
western Turkey

LYCIAN COAST

Europe Turkey
LYCIAN COAST

WHY GO *As summer fades, the sea is still at its warmest; perfect timing for a peaceful cruise around the rugged cliffs and shingle bays of Turkey's spectacular Lycian coast.*

Southwestern Turkey is home to more ancient ruins area-for-area than any other region in the world. Since time immemorial, conquerors, traders and travellers have beaten a path to these mighty monuments, set spectacularly on the crumbling hillsides, yet the sites still never fail to impress. Majestic and serene they loom over everything, colonized only by the wildflowers and butterflies that make their homes here. And what better way to see them than from a *gulet*, a traditional Turkish wooden sailing boat.

Sail smoothly past these wonders and pine-forested hillsides, as the sunlight dances on the surface of the turquoise sea, and you enjoy a meal of fresh fish cooked on board. Stop occasionally for a refreshing swim or to moor in a pretty little town. Around another spit of land, a sheltered cove or beautiful beach beckons from the foot of a towering cliff. The Mediterranean, set against the bleached blocks of old stone, looks almost luminous in its blueness as a couple of other *gulets* slowly drift by, shimmering and hazy in the heavy heat of the afternoon sun.

As the daylight begins to fade, coach parties vanish and the ruins are deserted once again. Highlighted against a darkening sky, the scenery seems as timeless and enduring today as it must have done millennia ago.

When Else to Go
April The weather is equally pleasant, and colourful spring flowers pepper the hillsides.

PLANNING YOUR TRIP **Getting there** International airports include Antalya, Bodrum, Dalaman and Izmir. **Getting around** *Gulet* (traditional Turkish boat) cruises can be booked in advance privately or as part of a group. **Weather** September has warm, sunny days. **Average temperature** 24°C / 75°F.

ANCIENT SITES

Ancient Lycia once comprised 19 mountain cities. The ruins and antiquities of these strongholds are today stunning places to explore.

Myra *(above)* was an ancient Greek city, where citizens worshipped the goddess Artemis. The acropolis, baths and amphitheatre are all staggeringly beautiful; look for the carved mask reliefs in the theatre.

Pinara has a sense of mystery and makes for lovely exploration, with the scent of pines clinging to the air. The amphitheatre at the base of the ancient city is impressive, as are the tombs that pockmark the mountain sides.

Letoon was an ancient Greek sanctuary, where Leto and her children Apollo and Artemis were worshipped. Strewn about the scene, the ancient ruins are a romantic sight.

Xanthos was the capital of Ancient Lycia. The extensive site has a spectacular collection of ancient ruins *(below)*, including superb examples of Lycian tombs.

LONDON

Europe England
LONDON

WHY GO *As summer draws to a close, London still promises endless thrills, from fabulous festivals to behind-the-scenes tours.*

Built on pomp and ceremony, London is now a cosmopolitan capital of dizzying diversity. Wherever you go you'll find slices of life from every corner of the globe, from dazzling celebrations of Caribbean culture to unbeatable salt beef bagels on Brick Lane.

As the long summer comes to an end, London still fizzes with excitement. Days are warm, parks are mellow and the lively hum of busy pubs pours out onto pavements. There are the last weeks of outdoor theatre at Shakespeare's Globe; Proms in the Park brings the finale of the world's largest classical music festival to Hyde Park; and the Open House weekend offers a sneak peak inside some of the city's most exclusive addresses. What's more, many of the major museums and galleries are free, so there's no excuse not to soak up a bit of culture during your trip.

When Else to Go
December Christmas brings carol concerts, twinkling lights and a giant Christmas tree to Trafalgar Square.

PLANNING YOUR TRIP **Getting there** Most international flights arrive into Heathrow and Gatwick airports. St Pancras International connects to European high-speed railways. **Getting around** London Underground and buses are frequent and reliable. **Weather** Mild and pleasant with occasional showers. **Average temperature** 14°C / 57°F.

UNMISSABLE MARKETS

Whether you're on the hunt for fashion, flowers or street food, a visit to one of London's many markets is a must.

1 Spanning several streets and buildings, **Camden Market** deals in all things retro, including vintage fashion, vinyl and quirky collectables. There are also scores of food stalls dishing out authentic nosh from all over the world.

2 **Portobello Road** is home to London's liveliest street market. Browse antiques and bric-à-brac, plus food stalls, crafts, clothes and music. Visit on Saturday to see the market in full swing.

3 London's oldest food market is also its most atmospheric. **Borough Market** has over a hundred stalls selling high-quality produce from all over the country, as well as international specialities.

4 Londoners head east on Sunday mornings to peruse the teeming plant and flower market on **Columbia Road**. Each stall is a colourful cornucopia of all things horticultural.

5 Tiny **Maltby Street Market** is a favourite among locals. What it lacks in size, it more than makes up for in choice, with over 30 artisan food and drink traders.

Clockwise from top left
Local eateries spill out
onto London streets;
contrasting architecture in
the City; the grand galleries
of Tate Britain; a guard
stands to attention on Horse
Guards Parade

Above Crossing a walkway through the rainforest canopy in Sabah, northern Borneo

Left The Labuk Bay monkey sanctuary; a Bornean orangutan, Tanjung Puting National Park

BORNEO

Asia Indonesia
BORNEO

WHY GO *Borneo's rainforests burst with fruit at this time of year, tempting orangutans down from the tree canopy. Join a jungle tour to glimpse the king of the swingers and other incredible wildlife.*

With its rocky pinnacles and misty rainforests, raging rivers, mangrove-encrusted shores and coral reefs, Borneo is a living Eden. The third largest island in the world, it boasts a rich biodiversity and is home to around 15,000 species of flowering plants, including many rare orchids. Made up of Brunei, Malay and Indonesian enclaves, Borneo is the centre of evolution for many endemic forest species, including the Asian elephant, the Sumatran rhinoceros and the clouded leopard. The rainforest, home to trees that tower to 75 m (246 ft), is also the natural habitat of the endangered Bornean orangutan, while the surrounding coastal waters support a magnificent ecosystem that abounds with marine life, corals and species of turtle. Deforestation and the cultivation of palm oil continue to cause controversy, but pristine forests remain and are protected by conservation projects that rely on tourism.

Aside from jungle exploration, Borneo's incredible landscape also makes for great adventure sports, such as mountain climbing, rainforest trekking and river rafting. Consider climbing Mount Kinabalu – you'll need to allow two days to climb and descend the mountain. If the sky is clear, the views from the summit are amazing. Whatever your Borneo adventure entails, the island's scenery and wildlife is undeniably spectacular.

When Else to Go
April After the monsoon season, this is a great time for relaxing on the beaches and jungle trekking.

PLANNING YOUR TRIP **Getting there** Kota Kinabalu is the island's main entry point and Kota Kinabalu International Airport has regular flights from Kuala Lumpur and Singapore. Kuching International Airport is also well served. **Getting around** Buses connect the major sights. In towns, minibuses and taxis are usually plentiful. **Weather** Borneo enjoys a hot tropical climate with some showers at this time of year. **Average temperature** 30°C / 86°F.

BEIJING

Asia China
BEIJING

WHY GO *Old meets new in China's charismatic capital city.*
September's cooler temperatures are welcome relief after the
muggy heat of the summer months.

This vast, uncontainable city teems with people spilling out onto the streets to
embrace the mellow temperature of the new season. The sheer size of Beijing's
population is reflected in the monumental scale of the city's ancient imperial
palaces and temple complexes. Take the Forbidden City: between its four
towering walls, colossal courtyards linked by elaborate gateways are filled with
lavish buildings, their roofs topped by a gilt menagerie of dragons, phoenixes
and other mythological beasts.

   Not far from the busy streets and honking cars, there is tranquillity among
the city's ancient *hutongs*, meandering alleyways that are as old as the Forbidden
City and often accessible only by rickshaw or bike. These untidy lanes and their
timeless, crumbling courtyards form a communal living space for the locals
where they can sit out and observe the world going by, gossip with their neighbours, play with their pets – including the occasional Pekinese dog – and enjoy
games of chess, mahjong and cards. But what is a *hutong* today could well be a
skyscraper tomorrow, thanks to Beijing's insatiable appetite for change. The city's
burgeoning arts and dining scene is transforming this ancient city into a cosmopolitan metropolis. Will you begin with ancient history or contemporary culture?

When Else to Go
February Chinese New Year celebrations take place across the city. **April** Spring
brings milder weather, perfect for meandering the parks to see blossoming flowers.

PLANNING YOUR TRIP **Getting there** Beijing is served by Beijing Capital
Airport. A rail link connects the airport to the city and taxis are readily available. **Getting
around** Beijing has cheap and efficient transport options, including a subway, buses (with
announcements in English), taxis and, in tourist areas, rickshaws. **Weather** September sees
relief from the heat of summer, and the odd shower. **Average temperature** 20°C / 68°F.

The rooftops of Beijing's sprawling Forbidden City, with the modern city in the distance

Oceania New Zealand
QUEENSTOWN

QUEENSTOWN

WHY GO *It's spring on the South Island, and Queenstown's green valleys and snowcapped peaks offer all manner of outdoor activity.*

Welcome to Queenstown, the adventure capital of the world. This shoreside town is a vast natural theme park where thrill-seekers can enjoy bungee jumping, whitewater rafting, jet-boating and countless other head-rush experiences. The town is also a premier ski destination, a snow sports playground set amid spectacular scenery, with the last of the snow available at this time of year.

It's not all thrills and spills, however. Queenstown welcomes spring in September, providing ample opportunity for more relaxed time spent outdoors. The landscape around the town bursts with cherry blossom and daffodils, best enjoyed via a walk or a gentle bike ride. There are also a number of vineyards that open their doors and cellars in spring. Come the evening, join the Kiwis and dine al fresco, toasting the day's events with a crisp glass of the local Pinot Noir.

When Else to Go
June The ski season kicks off with the Winter Festival, a showcase of fireworks, music performances, comedy acts, sport competitions and so much more.

PLANNING YOUR TRIP **Getting there** International flights arrive into Christchurch Airport, where you can catch a domestic flight to Queenstown or hire a car. **Getting around** Walking is the best way to get around the town but a 4WD vehicle is recommended for beyond Queenstown. **Weather** Mild but layers are advised. **Average temperature** 13°C/ 55°F.

A snowboarder jumping on the slopes of Coronet Peak, Queenstown

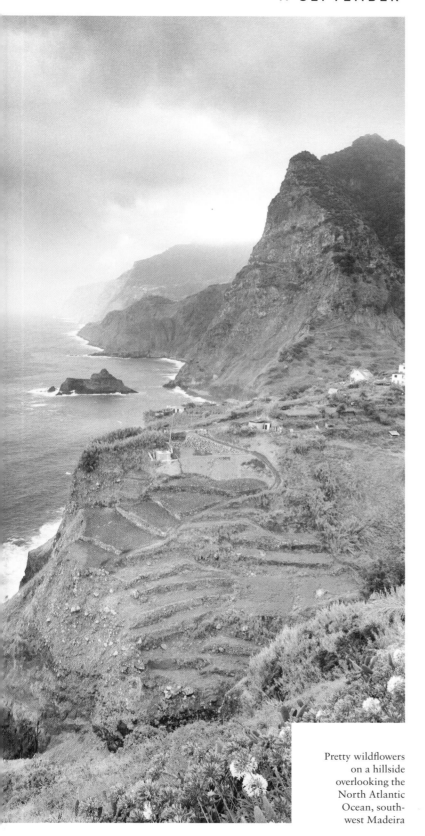

Pretty wildflowers on a hillside overlooking the North Atlantic Ocean, south-west Madeira

MADEIRA

Europe Portugal
MADEIRA

WHY GO *In September, the weather is at its best, the crowds have thinned and the countryside is blooming.*

Rising from the Atlantic like the mythical Atlantis, Madeira sits 1,000 km (620 miles) from Portugal's capital. In 1419, Portuguese adventurers exploring the coast of Africa recorded their fear as they headed for what they thought was the monster-infested rim of the ocean. What they found instead was paradise.

Lavishly decorated churches and luxurious rural mansions are the legacy of Madeira's early wealth. The scenery is as impressive as this art and architecture: you'll find tiny terraces clinging to the near-vertical valley sides, plus a plethora of tempting coves, forested ravines and exotic blooms. In September, as the colours of the landscape begin to change and visitors become fewer, Madeira has the air of a secret garden, just waiting to be discovered.

When Else to Go
February–March The Carnival of Madeira sees colourful costumes and parades just before Easter.

PLANNING YOUR TRIP **Getting there** Madeira International Airport is about 30 minutes from the capital, Funchal. Madeira is also a popular port of call for cruise liners. **Getting around** Buses reach most parts of the island but car hire gives flexibility. Taxis can be hired for day excursions. **Weather** Pleasantly warm with some showers. **Average temperature** 22°C / 72°F.

// OCTOBER

BUENOS AIRES, ARGENTINA   **196**

TUSCANY, ITALY   **198**   ALBUQUERQUE, USA   **206**

BUDAPEST, HUNGARY   **202**   CALIFORNIA COAST, USA   **208**

LOIRE VALLEY, FRANCE   **203**   OAXACA, MEXICO   **210**

QUEENSLAND, AUSTRALIA   **204**   KAUA'I, USA   **212**

The sun rising over the
sweeping purple-hued fields
of Tuscany's Val d'Orcia

BUENOS AIRES

South America Argentina
BUENOS AIRES

WHY GO *Warm, spring days coupled with fewer tourists makes October an ideal time for soaking up the diversity and cultural depth of Buenos Aires.*

Entwined with the city's sights, parks, restaurants and nightlife is something more intangible. You'll find it brushed in sensual strokes by tango dancers across the cobbled streets of the *barrios* (neighbourhoods) of San Telmo and La Boca. Passionate fans shout it out from the bleachers in soccer stadiums. It drifts in the smoke of roasting meat at a *parrilla* (steak house) and shimmers in a glass of Argentina's renowned wine. Eva Perón embodied it back in the late 1940s and early 1950s. And the *porteños* (inhabitants of Buenos Aires) who patronize the trendy restaurants along the riverfront *barrio* of Puerto Madero and fill the bohemian bars in Palermo Viejo give it a contemporary twist.

Buenos Aires combines European style and sophistication with the South American gift of knowing how to have a good time. Come and see for yourself how this city mirrors the irrepressible spirit of Argentina.

When Else to Go
August Put on your dancing shoes at the World Tango Festival, a two-week event celebrating Argentina's famous dance.

PLANNING YOUR TRIP **Getting there** Flights arrive into Ezeiza International Airport, 35 km (22 miles) from the city centre. **Getting around** The *subte* (metro) and buses are efficient; use taxis at night. **Weather** Warm, with plenty of sun. **Average temperature** 20°C / 68°F.

Left Dusk falling on colourful buildings and trees lining a pretty square in the historic *barrio* of La Boca

Below A sign for a tango bar in Buenos Aires, one of many in the city

Cypress trees and
cultivated hills in the
beautiful Val d'Orcia

TUSCANY

Europe Italy
TUSCANY

WHY GO *Harvest time sees the rolling Tuscan hillsides draped in sunburned shades and romantic autumnal mists.*

Tuscany is a feast for the senses. Sublime art and breathtaking architecture vie for attention amid incomparably romantic landscapes. But in October it's the region's rustic flavours that take centre stage. This is the season when porcini mushrooms and prized *tartufo* (truffles) flavour risottos and game appears on local menus – slow-stewed wild boar, or hare cooked with red wine and herbs, served with the region's wide pappardelle pasta.

Each area has its own speciality. Think of *bistecca alla fiorentina* – thick steak from the Valdiciana, drizzled with the finest olive oil and grilled over a chestnut-wood fire; Prato's *cantucci*, biscuits dipped in sweet Vin Santo; and *pici* pasta from the hill towns around Siena. Discover these authentic flavours as you tour the serene Tuscan countryside, or join a local cookery course and learn the secrets behind this region's sublime cuisine.

When Else to Go
May Enjoy balmy days, quiet beaches and the many *sagre* (local food festivals) in the countryside.

PLANNING YOUR TRIP **Getting there** Tuscany's main airports are in Florence and Pisa. **Getting around** In cities, walk or use public transport. Hire a car to tour the countryside. **Weather** Warm, but be prepared for rain and mist. **Average temperature** 20°C / 68°F.

A TASTE OF TUSCANY

1 **Cooking experiences** Boost your culinary credentials at one of the region's many cooking courses. Stop by San Lorenzo food market in Florence for a tour and pasta-making masterclass.

2 **Florentine street food** Traditionally made with tripe, *lampredotto* is Florence's most popular street food. Head to Nencioni on Piazza Mercato Nuovo to sample the best in town.

3 **White truffle market of Crete Senesi** Sleepy San Giovanni D'Asso springs to life during the white truffle season (November). Eat your fill of truffles at this market fair.

4 **Sagra della Bistecca** Every Tuscan town has its own food festivals (*sagre*), but not one beats Cortona's steak festival. Held every year in mid-August, it is the region's most important gastronomic event.

5 **Fine dining** Tuscany is home to some 35 Michelin-starred restaurants, where utterly delicious dishes are also feasts for the eyes *(below)*.

Bridges straddling
Florence's River Arno as
the sun sets over the city

Europe Hungary
BUDAPEST

WHY GO *As golden leaves colour tree-lined terraces and the summer crowds begin to fade, join the locals in some good, clean fun.*

Straddling both sides of the Danube, Hungary's capital is not one city but two. To the west, the medieval streets and imperial palaces of Buda; to the east, Pest, the commercial and political hub. Here, astoundingly ornate architecture abounds, a hark back to the Austro-Hungarian heyday, while grimy ruin bars are a staple of the city's nightlife.

Perhaps the biggest draw are the numerous thermal bathhouses. For a fizzing soak in an upmarket riot of Art Nouveau expression, head to the Gellért Baths. Or you may prefer the more humble Széchenyi Baths. Here, on the Pest side of town, you'll make waves with ordinary folk as they enjoy their daily treat – a hot bath, a game of chess and a bottle of beer. Indulge in an invigorating massage, to help you really get under the skin of this city.

BUDAPEST

When Else to Go
April This is a great time to experience Hungarian folk traditions including painting eggs at Easter. The weather is pleasant and the city isn't yet overcrowded.

PLANNING YOUR TRIP **Getting there** International flights arrive into Ferenc Liszt Airport. **Getting around** Metro, buses, trams and taxis operate throughout the city. **Weather** Mostly dry and sunny. **Average temperature** 16°C / 61°F.

Aerial view of Széchenyi Baths, the biggest bath complex in Europe

The grand Château
de Chenonceau,
shrouded in an
eerie fog, seemingly
floating on the
water's still surface

LOIRE VALLEY

Europe France
LOIRE VALLEY

WHY GO *Explore French splendour in relative tranquillity as summer coach tours diminish.*

European architecture doesn't get richer than the grand *châteaux* of the Loire Valley, circled by their historic moats. Reflecting the decadent beauty of the Renaissance, more than 50 15th- and 16th-century wildly extravagant mansions pepper the region.

Yet the Loire Valley is not just about stunning art and architecture. Dubbed "the Garden of France", the Loire is celebrated for its glorious gastronomy. Look out for local apples and pears, and, of course, the products of the Loire grapes, including great white wines such as Muscadet, Pouilly-Fumé and Sancerre. Venture into troglodyte caves around Vouvray, Saumur and Angers – home to the famous Saumur button mushrooms that fill the markets, where you can assemble a delectable picnic to enjoy as you tour this abundant region.

When Else to Go
May Early summer sees a little less rainfall and warmer days – perfect for a cycling trip.

PLANNING YOUR TRIP **Getting there** The area is served by two airports – Nantes-Atlantique and Tours Val de Loire. **Getting around** Public transport is limited. Join a boat tour, cycle or hire a car. **Weather** Mild, but be prepared for light rain. **Average temperature** 16°C / 60°F.

QUEENSLAND ISLAND ESCAPES

Scattered all along Queensland's coast are picture-perfect islands, with pristine beaches and stunning coral reefs. Here are four of our favourites.

Fraser Island Known as *K'gari* (meaning paradise) by local Aboriginal people, the world's largest sand island doesn't disappoint, with its gorgeous white beaches, lush rainforests and clear lakes. You're also likely to encounter dingos, the island's most famous residents.

Lizard Island This remote island can only be reached by private charter. Located on the Great Barrier Reef between the inner and outer reef systems, the diving and snorkelling opportunities here are unparalleled. The underwater world is a kaleidoscope of colour.

Heron Island Wildlife is everywhere here. The island's pisonia trees are home to thousands of birds, including noddy terns and muttonbirds. Between October and March, you can watch green and loggerhead turtles make their way up the beach to nest.

Whitsunday Island The highlight of this island *(below)* is the breathtaking Whitehaven Beach. Recognized as one of the world's best beaches, it has 9 km (6 miles) of pure white sand.

QUEENSLAND

Oceania Australia
QUEENSLAND

WHY GO *October is a great time to visit Australia's adventure playground. It's fairly quiet and the weather is perfect – warm, pleasant and ideal for long days spent outdoors.*

Queensland ticks all the boxes for a sunny holiday destination, with soft white-sand beaches and island hideaways; though thrill-seekers may think that lounging around is a waste given the endless world-class adventure possibilities.

The coast overflows with opportunities for getting in and about the water, whether you are looking to go island hopping on a gleaming yacht or to delve deep below sea level on a scuba dive. Divers bubble back to the surface from the Great Barrier Reef enthusing about the spectacular delights encountered below.

Inland, lush rainforests await. Venture into the dense foliage and another Queensland unfolds, as exotic animal calls shriek out among ancient trees. Even here, activities are in abundance – tumble down raging rivers on a raft, ride the rapids on a kayak or even fling yourself off a ridiculous height with only a rubber bungee for company.

When Else to Go
September Queensland's capital has an unbeatable buzz during the Brisbane Festival, with theatre, music, dance and circus shows.

The famous Heart Reef, part of the Great Barrier Reef, in the azure waters of Queensland's Whitsundays

PLANNING YOUR TRIP **Getting there** Flights arrive into Cairns and Brisbane. **Getting around** Hire a car or use the public buses. **Weather** Warm days and cool nights. **Average temperature** 25°C / 77°F.

ALBUQUERQUE

Right Admiring hundreds of colourful balloons as they drift gracefully across the desert sky

Below A balloon illuminated by its glowing burner; fiesta crowds enjoying the atmosphere

North America USA
ALBUQUERQUE

WHY GO *Held every October, the mass ascension of hundreds of multicoloured hot-air balloons at Albuquerque International Balloon Fiesta never fails to leave onlookers breathless.*

It's a romantic picture – a single hot-air balloon sailing gracefully and silently across the sky. There's something uniquely enchanting about ballooning; the huge colourful orb just hangs in the air as if by magic. If one balloon is magical, seeing hundreds of them dotting the sky in an endless canvas of abstract shapes and vivid colours is beyond words. This is what happens every year at the thrilling Albuquerque International Balloon Fiesta, the largest convention of hot-air balloons in the world.

Those hoping to catch the best of the action rise at the crack of dawn, when more than 500 balloons in shapes previously unimagined lift off simultaneously, filling the barren desert sky as the crowds gaze in amazement from below. When you're not staring up at the spectacle, weave your way through countless docked balloons, chat with pilots, capture breathtaking photographs and sample traditional New Mexican fare, such as warm, puffy Navajo frybread and steaming tortilla soup, enjoying live music and entertainment as you eat. As night descends on the Rio Grande Valley, stand in awe of the Balloon Glow, as hundreds of balloons on the ground are illuminated all at once from the glow of their burners. Once the field clears, a spectacular fireworks display wraps up the evening with a bang.

When Else to Go
February Skiers visit Albuquerque to enjoy the slopes of the nearby Sandia Mountains.

PLANNING YOUR TRIP **Getting there** Balloon Fiesta Park is around 19 km (12 miles) north of Albuquerque Sunport, the state's only major airport. **Getting around** Most visitors rely on hire cars or the ABQ Ride bus system. The New Mexico Rail Runner shuttles people to and from the park. **Weather** Generally dry. Cool in the morning and warm in the afternoon. **Average temperature** 21°C / 70°F.

MONTEREY

SANTA BARBARA

North America USA
CALIFORNIA COAST

WHY GO *California's Highway 1 is hard to beat for driving pleasure, with the stretch from Monterey to Santa Barbara the most thrilling. The road is much quieter at this time of year.*

Highway 1 snakes along wave-lashed seashores, hugging the Golden State's coast all the way from the beautiful vineyards of Mendocino to just south of the sprawling metropolis of LA. Pick up a hire car in San Francisco and drive south 200 km (120 miles) to Monterey for the start of the most famous stretch of the drive. It's a classic route that winds on for 400 km (250 miles) to surf-city Santa Barbara. Along the way you'll pass picturesque seaside towns, forests of towering redwoods and Spanish missions that pre-date the state's founding. One minute you're skimming alongside a golden beach caressed by smoothly curving sets of waves and the next you're looking down onto thundering surf. But the drama really begins as you wind along the spectacularly scenic Big Sur, where waves smash ashore at the base of soaring mountains.

The landscape softens further south; the mountains move inland and cypress redwoods give way to palm trees and bougainvillea. Santa Barbara slips into view with its Spanish-style homes and surfer-dude chic. You'll have earned some rest and relaxation after a few days of driving, so enjoy some beach time here in Santa Barbara, indulge in a winery tour and raise a glass of crisp local Chardonnay.

When Else to Go

April–May Great weather and quieter beaches before the summer starts.

Crashing waves and foaming surf along a rugged outcrop of the beautiful Big Sur, California

PLANNING YOUR TRIP **Getting there** San Francisco and LAX are both busy international airports, and are well connected to their respective cities by train, bus and taxi. **Getting around** Hiring a car is the best option, although buses and Amtrak's Coast Starlight trains operate between LA and San Francisco. **Weather** Usually sunny and warm, although it can get quite hot inland. **Average temperature** 25°C / 77°F.

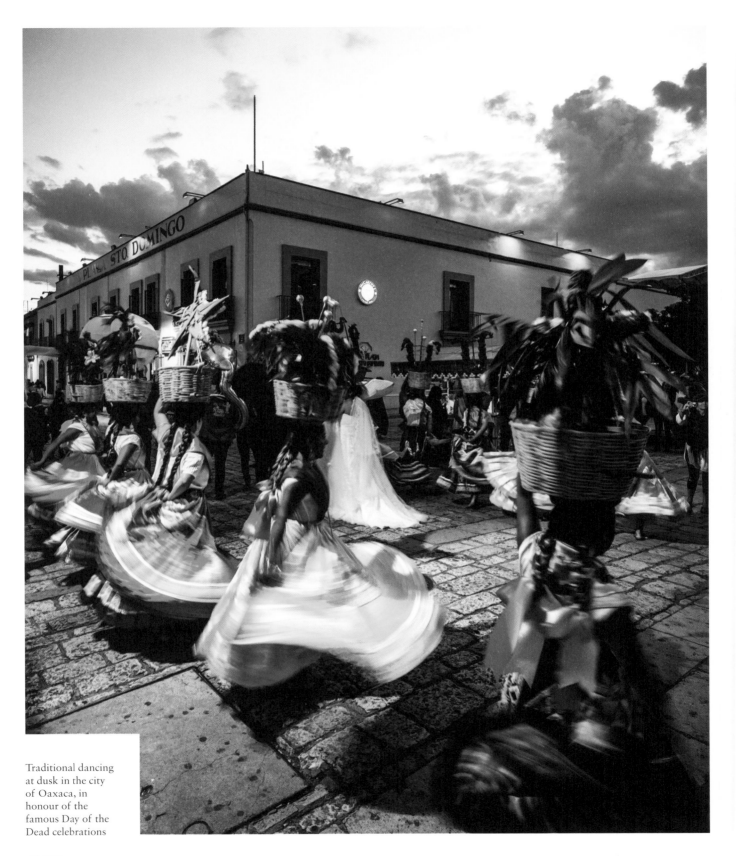

Traditional dancing at dusk in the city of Oaxaca, in honour of the famous Day of the Dead celebrations

CITY HIGHLIGHTS

Cool and cultural, Oaxaca rivals the best of Latin America's cities. Here's how.

1

Gorgeous architecture in the form of Baroque churches and colourful, colonial-era buildings circle cobbled plazas.

2

Street art and bohemian bars abound. Embark on a hunt for murals by the likes of revered Lapiztola before evening tequilas.

3

Numerous markets sell freshly ground coffee, local mezcal, gorgeous woven baskets and embroidered clothing. Perfect souvenirs.

Central America Mexico

OAXACA

WHY GO *Oaxaca is the best place to see Mexico's Day of the Dead celebrations, from 31 October to 2 November.*

This most Mexican of fiestas is a truly supernatural event where the dead are believed to return to earth to commune with their living relatives. In the colonial city of Oaxaca and its surrounding indigenous villages, these ancient beliefs thrive and the celebrations are at their most vivid. The reunion between the living and the dead is both joyful and poignant, and the atmosphere can be amazingly animated. To welcome their late relatives, families decorate loved ones' graves with flowers, candles and miniature skulls. They spend hours in graveyards communing with the deceased, even staying for night-long vigils. The sight of a cemetery glittering with candles and buzzing with chatter, and the dancing that accompany these reunions, will stay with you.

When Else to Go

July The Guelaguetza festival celebrates Oaxaca's indigenous communities with parades and performances.

PLANNING YOUR TRIP **Getting there** Oaxaca is 400 km (250 miles) southeast of Mexico City, with most travellers arriving via a domestic flight from Mexico City. **Getting around** There are plenty of taxis and buses. **Weather** Warm with the odd shower. **Average temperature** 25°C / 77°F.

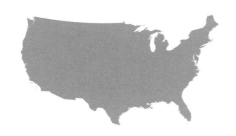

KAUA'I

North America USA
KAUA'I

WHY GO *The Hawaiian island of Kaua'i is all about the sea and the lush green nature inland. With the summer crowds gone, October is the perfect time to kick back and indulge in this tropical paradise.*

Kaua'i, nicknamed the "Garden Island", is covered with dense forests and myriad colourful flowers; it echoes with the twittering welcome of exotic birds while the hypnotic boom of waves crashing onto the golden beaches draws you in. Once a volcano rising from the sea, the island evolved into a breathtaking combination of rainforest, deserts, plains and mountains. It is home to the Waimea Canyon, the largest canyon in the Pacific, and the Nā Pali Coast, featuring jungle-clad cliffs rising sharply from dark blue sea. Kaua'i is an intriguing place, created by the immense forces of nature, and is still subject to them. Hollywood agrees and has used the unruly, primeval landscape as a back-drop in several films, including *King Kong* and *Jurassic World*.

The mountains, canyons and beaches, especially on the Nā Pali Coast, are truly unique. To get a spectacular sea view, join a kayak tour and paddle round until the Nā Pali cliffs rear high above you. As you glide through the water you'll be confronted with the same breathtaking spectacle the first Polynesians saw when they stumbled upon this natural paradise.

When Else to Go
September The Kaua'i Marathon and the Kaua'i Mokihana Festival, a week-long celebration of Hawaiian culture, take place.

PLANNING YOUR TRIP **Getting there** Flights from the US mainland arrive in Lihu'e, the main city on Kaua'i. **Getting around** Hiring a car is the best option. **Weather** October is warm; rainfall is frequent but short-lived. **Average temperature** 24°C / 75°F.

Sunshine dappling the jungle-clad cliffs of the Nā Pali Coast, with gentle waves lapping the golden shore

// NOVEMBER

VIETNAM   **216**

TOKYO, JAPAN   **218**   AITUTAKI, COOK ISLANDS   **224**

BURGUNDY, FRANCE   **220**   TASMANIA, AUSTRALIA   **226**

MISSISSIPPI CRUISE, USA   **221**   BAHAMAS   **228**

SEOUL, SOUTH KOREA   **222**   RAJASTHAN, INDIA   **230**

A riot of shining
neon lights in Shinjuku,
central Tokyo

VIETNAM

Asia
VIETNAM

WHY GO *With both captivating cities and time-forgotten countryside, Vietnam always rewards exploration. The start of the dry season brings uninterrupted pleasant days.*

With a blend of mesmerizing sights, sounds, smells and tastes that is like no other, Vietnam delivers adventure and sensory overload. This is a land of picture-postcard images: a scattering of bobbing conical straw hats dotting a patchwork landscape of emerald rice fields; graceful girls in their elegant *ao dai* dresses, zipping around cities on motorcycles; and the dizzying colours of a Cao Dai temple. From a rich civilization with deeply held traditions has risen a country that has seen the future, and rushed headlong into it. The past, however, is always remembered, whether it be at ancient temples or the poignant sites of terrible 20th-century wars.

In contrast to other parts of Vietnam, the Mekong Delta seems untouched. The pace of life is slow in this lush, watery world of rice paddies, fish farms and floating markets, where an intricate web of canals links tiny green islands on which all manner of tropical fruits grow.

Noisy, vibrant, chaotic and colourful, Ho Chi Minh City dazzles, with its French colonial architecture and striking modern buildings. Tiny cafés line traffic-clogged streets, the smells of aromatic spices waft from countless restaurants and food stalls. Have a drink at the balcony bar of a high-rise hotel, and watch the city explode in a riot of neon – then get down there and join in.

When Else to Go
January–February Take part in Vietnam's extravagant Tet (Lunar New Year) celebrations.

Above Farmers walking through the terraced rice fields of Mu Cang Chai in northeast Vietnam

Right A boat paddling through the Mekong Delta; dining out in Ho Chi Minh City

PLANNING YOUR TRIP **Getting there** Hanoi is served by Nội Bài International Airport and Ho Chi Minh City has Tân Son Nhất International Airport. **Getting around** Cyclos, *xe om* (motorbikes) and taxis zip around the towns; buses, trains and planes cover longer distances. **Weather** Dry, but humidity is high. **Average temperature** 27°C / 81°F.

PICTURE PERFECT

1 **Tokyu Plaza Omotesando Harajuku** Snap a kaleidoscope-like image of this multistory shopping complex from the top of the mirror-encased escalator as you exit.

2 **Nakagin Capsule Tower** Take a picture of this modular building from across the street. Resembling a stack of washing machines, it's a rare example of Japanese Metabolism.

3 **Shibuya Crossing** Grab a coffee at Shibuya Tsutaya's glass-fronted Starbucks, then make a beeline for the second floor, the best place to get a shot of the famous Shibuya Crossing.

4 **Golden Gai** Home to a maze of 200 tiny bars, the six narrow alleyways of Golden Gai are like a portal to a distant time. Venture here after dark to snap photos of buzzy bar life.

5 **Sensō-ji Temple** Open 24 hours a day, you can capture this peaceful Buddhist temple complex *(below)* at all hours. Come just before dawn for the perfect shot of the sun rising over the Kaminarimon (Thunder Gate).

Bright and colourful neon signs overlooking a busy zebra crossing in the ward of Shinjuku, in Tokyo

TOKYO

Asia Japan
TOKYO

WHY GO *With pleasant days, clear skies and a stunning backdrop of golden foliage, November is a great time to visit this modern metropolis where the past and future collide.*

Nowhere in the world combines the ancient and modern quite like Tokyo. On the one hand, it's a futuristic neon cityscape, fast-paced and crowded, with a high-octane life-style. Think swarms of worker-bees crossing the Shibuya intersection, all of them talking into high-tech mobile phones while animated advertising hoardings bombard them with strobe-effect slogans. On the other hand, there are quiet cobbled side streets leading to secluded Shinto shrines and Buddhist temples, where Tokyoites can grab a rare moment of quiet contemplation, before continuing with their busy daily lives.

While shopping, dining and the bright lights of the entertainment district remain the superficial attractions of big-city Tokyo life, the most rewarding experiences are far simpler: admiring the chrysanthemums on a walk in the Imperial Palace East Garden, eating a hearty bowl of noodles at a street-side stall and watching children play with autumn leaves at a backstreet shrine. Such sights are a humble reminder that while Tokyo appears to be the ultimate 21st-century city, bustling and jostling into the future, scratch beneath its brash veneer and you'll soon see that the traditional

values of Japanese society – nature, family and philosophy – are still very much alive.

When Else to Go
March–April Instead of autumn leaves, you'll find delicate cherry blossoms in Tokyo's parks.

PLANNING YOUR TRIP **Getting there** Narita International Airport is 66 km (40 miles) from downtown. **Getting around** The extensive underground system is cheap and efficient. **Weather** Cool and dry. **Average temperature** 15°C / 59°F.

Yakitori restaurants on Memory Lane in Tokyo

BURGUNDY

Europe France
BURGUNDY

WHY GO *Take a cruise on this golden region's canals at harvest time to sample its bountiful delights, from fiery mustard to warming wine.*

Brimming with good food and fine wine, Burgundy is France's heartiest region. In November the hunting season is underway, mushrooms are being gathered and the grape harvest is being celebrated, making it the perfect time to chug along the 242-km (150-mile) Canal de Bourgogne in a canal boat, stopping off at tasting rooms, picturesque villages and idyllic picnic spots.

Alternatively, cycle or stroll through the burnished gold forests and ruddy vineyards. Once you've worked up an appetite, sample Dijon's famous mustard, comforting *boeuf bourguignon* or wild mushrooms, newly gathered, all washed down with a glass of Chablis, Côte de Nuits or Côte de Beaune.

When Else to Go
July The Festival International d'Opéra Baroque sees Baune host operas, concerts and recitals every weekend.

PLANNING YOUR TRIP **Getting there** Dijon's airport is 6 km (4 miles) south of the city. Canal tours depart from Paris and Dijon. **Getting around** Apart from by canal, the main towns are linked by bus. **Weather** Cold in the evenings. **Average temperature** 6°C / 43°F.

The *Queen of the Mississippi* in early morning mist

Autumn mist blanketing a vineyard in Burgundy

North America USA
MISSISSIPPI CRUISE

NEW ORLEANS

WHY GO *Mild weather makes autumn the perfect time to enjoy both the river and onshore activities to the full without the summer's humidity.*

The mighty Mississippi is the largest river in the US. Countless literary and musical masterpieces have been inspired by it over the years, but the true folklife of America has its roots firmly grounded in the lower Mississippi. From New Orleans, as you cruise along the river, the history of the South unfolds.

The elegantly appointed, six-deck *Queen of the Mississippi* paddlewheel steamboat makes the journey from the port of New Orleans to Oak Alley Plantation – the grand residence used in the opening scene of the Deep South classic *Gone With the Wind*. Then she sails on to the quaint town of Natchez, where you can hop straight off the boat into 19th-century

America. Packed with history, this is the oldest European settlement on the Mississippi River. The next stop is historic Vicksburg, Mississippi, where the National Military Park captures the spirit of the Civil War. Explore the Vicksburg battlefield where more than 1,300 monuments, fortifications and a restored Union gunboat tell the story of those that lost their lives here.

Further down river lies Baton Rouge, Louisiana's sleepy state capital, where historic buildings reflect the city's French Creole roots. Soon it's time to return to the 21st century as the boat chugs back to New Orleans and the bustling streets of the French Quarter.

When Else to Go
February–March During Mardi Gras, New Orleans becomes one big party.

PLANNING YOUR TRIP Getting there New Orleans is a good place to start a cruise and is served by Louis Armstrong International Airport. **Getting around** Tours from the cruise are included as part of the *Queen of the Mississippi* package. **Weather** Mainly clear. **Average temperature** 16°C / 61°F.

Bukchon Hanok
Village, with
Seoul's modern
buildings and
mountains beyond

SEOUL

Asia South Korea
SEOUL

WHY GO *Seoul has soul in November. While the city pulses, the surrounding mountains provide a peaceful retreat, with walking trails and trees ablaze with the colours of autumn.*

Seoul is a city of contrasts, where glimmering skyscrapers loom above timeless Buddhist temples and leafy parks. The capital distils the essence of everything that is enchanting about South Korea. Days spent exploring the traditional streets of Bukchon Hanok and art galleries of Leeum Samsung turn into nights necking *soju* in a rooftop bar, with K-pop providing a thumping soundtrack.

All the while, standing silent guard as the city rushes on, are Seoul's mighty mountains, their forested slopes a playground for walkers. November is the perfect time to get out in nature – the humid summer has given way to pleasantly cool autumn weather, and the forested hills erupt in a riot of fiery reds, yellows and ambers. Bukhansan is criss-crossed with gentle forest trails that reward your efforts with incredible views of the metropolis. Sound too

much like hard work? Namsan, in the heart of the city, combines stellar views over the city with the added convenience of a cable car. If you prefer to stay closer to sea level, stroll the riverside boardwalks of Hangang Park, or get lost amid the trees, lakes and flowers of Seoul Forest.

You'll have worked up an appetite after all that fresh air and Seoul's celebrated food scene won't disappoint, especially as November welcomes the Seoul Kimchi Festival, with street stalls serving up bowls of the spicy delicacy. Day or night, mountains or megalopolis, South Korea's capital is utterly spellbinding.

When Else to Go
April Pink cherry blossom blankets temples and parks. **December** The snow-covered temples and palaces are particularly atmospheric.

PLANNING YOUR TRIP **Getting there** Seoul is served by Incheon International Airport, around 48 km (30 miles) from the city, and is connected by AREX train, bus and taxi. **Getting around** A subway system connects most neighbourhoods and there are trains and buses. **Weather** Fairly cool with some rainfall. **Average temperature** 7°C / 45°F.

PARKS AND WALKING TRAILS

1 **Seoul Forest** was opened in 2005 as a symbol of Seoul's commitment to green space. It is a great spot for a stroll or bike ride.

2 **Banpo Hangang Park** is loved for the technicolour Banpo Bridge Rainbow Fountain and is popular for *chimaek* – fried chicken and beer.

3 The **Changdeokgung grounds** were the pleasure gardens of kings in a bygone era, and today the palace grounds remain a peaceful sanctuary.

4 **Namsan Park** represents Seoul's contrasts: rich in trees, trails and wildlife, but crested by the modern N Seoul Tower.

5 **Bukhansan National Park** *(below)* has winding mountain trails, which make for lovely hiking, especially along the fortress walls.

AITUTAKI

Oceania Cook Islands
AITUTAKI

WHY GO *The end of "winter" in the Cook Islands is the perfect time to visit this technicolour paradise, without the threat of rain dampening your spirits.*

It's said that the Cook Islands, and particularly Aitutaki, are what Tahiti was 50 years ago; a place of such beauty and purity that it cannot fail to fill visitors with complete awe.

Aitutaki sits at the apex of a vast lagoon dotted by tiny islands called *motus*. "Blue" is the colour usually applied to South Sea water but Aitutaki only begins at "blue" – the lagoon forms a quilt of unmodulated patches in every shade imaginable of blue and green: emerald, aquamarine, cobalt, Prussian blue, royal blue and periwinkle. Below the water, the colour palette turns psychedelic with vivid corals that are only eclipsed by resident fish that seem to have dipped themselves in a paintbox: reds, oranges, royal blues, canary yellows, turquoise – sometimes all on the same fish. On land, this riot continues: the bold, seductive reds of the immortelle trees; the woven floral crowns that people wear in their hair; and the sensual shades and perfumes in the

The crystal clear waters and white sands of the lagoon framing Aitutaki

leis (flower garlands) thrown around visitors' necks when they arrive in this painting brought to life.

When Else to Go
September See humpback whales close to shore as they pass by the Cook Islands on their journey to warmer waters.

PLANNING YOUR TRIP **Getting there** Air Rarotonga has daily flights to Aitutaki from the international airport on Rarotonga. **Getting around** You can easily explore on foot, but cars, scooters and bikes can be hired. **Weather** Warm and dry. **Average temperature** 29°C / 84°F.

SNORKELLING SPOTS

An abundance of marine life and colourful coral landscapes thrive in the underwater world that separates the Cook Islands from one another, making the scenery beneath the water's surface just as impressive as that on dry land.

---

1 **Aroa Lagoon Marine Reserve**, on the main island of Rarotonga, is home to impressive reefs.

2 Isolated **Muri Lagoon** is only reachable by kayak from Muri Beach, but it's worth the journey.

3 Sheltered **Aitutaki Lagoon** is known for its clear waters and sheer abundance of colourful sea life.

4 The volcanic landscape of **Black Rock**, Rarotonga, looks otherworldly from beneath the water.

5 **One Foot Island**, near Aitutaki, is an underwater metropolis due to its deep channels.

TASMANIA

Oceania Australia
TASMANIA

WHY GO *With mild spring days, blooming wildflowers and long daylight hours, this is the ideal time to pack your bags, don your hiking boots and discover what "Tassie" has to offer.*

It's easy to feel humbled by the enormity of Tasmania's wild and remote location. Virtually at the edge of the world, there's just the vast expanse of the mighty Southern Ocean separating this spectacular tract of wilderness from the Antarctic continent. To the west, it's some 20,000 km (12,000 miles) to the next landmass – South America. Such isolation has been a lifeline for the island's native flora and fauna, and the island has millions of hectares of wild countryside to explore.

Tasmania is covered in managed walking tracks, including the famed Overland Track – a 65-km (40-mile) six-day walk through its rugged alpine heart. On the Freycinet Peninsula, the short but thoroughly rewarding 45-minute uphill trek to the Wineglass Bay Lookout provides a heart-stopping view of one of the planet's most spectacular stretches of sand.

On the west of the island, in the glacial lakes and streams of the Franklin-Gordon Wild Rivers National Park, there are links with the Permian period, some 250 million years ago. Primitive crustaceans still live here among the rivers and ferns they've called home for millions of years. The Franklin River, one of three major rivers that run through the park, is revered by Tasmanians for its natural, cultural and historical significance. Experience its beauty and isolation on a rafting excursion with a local guide.

Off the usual tourist trail, Tasmania is Australia's best-kept secret, offering endless possibilities for adventure in an ancient landscape that teems with life.

When Else to Go
January Summer is festival time, with foodies' favourite Taste of Tasmania and the pumping Falls Festival, MONA FOMA and Cygnet Folk Festival.

PLANNING YOUR TRIP **Getting there** There are flights to Hobart from Melbourne, Adelaide, Sydney, Brisbane and Canberra. Ferries make regular overnight journeys from Melbourne to Devonport on the north coast. **Getting around** Touring is best done with a car. **Weather** Generally warm and dry. **Average temperature** 20°C / 68°F.

A path winding through the wonderfully wild scenery of Cradle Mountain National Park, Tasmania

BAHAMAS

Caribbean
BAHAMAS

WHY GO *Fringed by pristine sand and teal-blue lagoons, the Bahamas are a beachgoer's delight in November. For the more adventurous, there is so much more to be discovered.*

This chain of tranquil isles – some large, others tiny – is sprinkled across a vast area of blue-green western Atlantic waters. Each group is as distinct as a thumbprint. Island-hopping from one to the next, visitors discover that even the most Lilliputian island is blessed with gargantuan charm.

Nassau, the capital, with its plethora of hotels and restaurants, provides a perfect combination of fine beaches and aquatic adventures that appeal to the young and young-at-heart. Choose from a range of activities – from aqua-biking to sunfish-boat sailing – at Cable Beach. You can even take to the air for a bird's-eye view of Nassau and neighbouring Paradise Island.

Once you've had your fill of energetic escapades, it's time to hit the beach for some much-needed down time. There are, of course, plenty to choose from, but few can rival Eleuthera's Harbour Island, or Briland as it's known to locals, famous for its pink sands merging into the electric-blue water. One of the Family Islands, Briland, with its pastel clapboard cottages, is the ultimate picture-postcard. Peek into its tiny churches, indulge in traditional seafood restaurants and hire a golf cart to explore the island. And after all that, submerge yourself in the turquoise waters and soak up that hot Bahamian sun.

When Else to Go
January Junkanoo, the mother of all street parties, takes place across the islands on New Year's Day.

PLANNING YOUR TRIP **Getting there** Fly into Lynden Pindling International Airport, then board domestic flights, ferries and mailboats to reach the other islands. **Getting around** There are many modes of transport around the islands, including car, boat and hired bicycles. Taxis are readily available. **Weather** Sunny with cooling trade winds. **Average temperature** 26°C / 79°F.

A wooden pier stretching out from Pink Sands Beach

RAJASTHAN

Asia India
RAJASTHAN

WHY GO *The summer heat has passed, making this the perfect time to discover the legacy of the magical state of Rajasthan. Journey through gorgeous scenery on board the Palace on Wheels train.*

A majestic land of fairy-tale palaces and vibrant local life, Rajasthan fulfils all expectations of India. There is no more appropriate way of travelling through India than by train, and the opulent Palace on Wheels provides a truly unforgettable journey from Delhi to Agra. Chugging leisurely through Rajasthan allows you to revel in the scenery, comprising lush fields, tropical forests and stunning palaces.

This land is home to rajas and maharajas, and their culture and history will delight curious travellers who wish to experience India's past and present. In this desert kingdom, fortresses wrap themselves around hills, while in the plains below pleasure gardens surround serene lakeside fortresses. Passing through the ornate gates of Rajasthan's palaces means stepping into a world that encompasses the folk traditions and vivid history of this enchanting state. Here you'll discover treasures that tell stories of those who have peopled these historic abodes through the generations. Luxury still pervades, even today; meander through marble hallways, indulge in fine cuisine and admire the exquisite heirlooms found at every turn.

The pace of the Palace on Wheels journey provides ample time to explore the state's memorable palaces and unwind in your own lavish cabin, or socialize with a cocktail in the sumptuous dining carriage. On board this luxurious train, you're in for a journey of a lifetime.

When Else to Go
March Rajasthan celebrates Gangaur, a festival honouring Gauri or Parvati, the Hindu goddess of fertility, love, beauty and marriage.

PLANNING YOUR TRIP **Getting there** Delhi's Indira Gandhi International Airport, in the state of Uttar Pradesh, is the main entry point, though Jaipur and Jodhpur both have airports. **Getting around** There are regular trains from Delhi to cities and towns throughout Rajasthan. The Palace on Wheels travels from Delhi through Rajasthan and onto Agra between October and March. Towns and cities have taxis, cycle rickshaws and auto rickshaws. **Weather** Dry with a more bearable heat. **Average temperature** 33°C / 91°F.

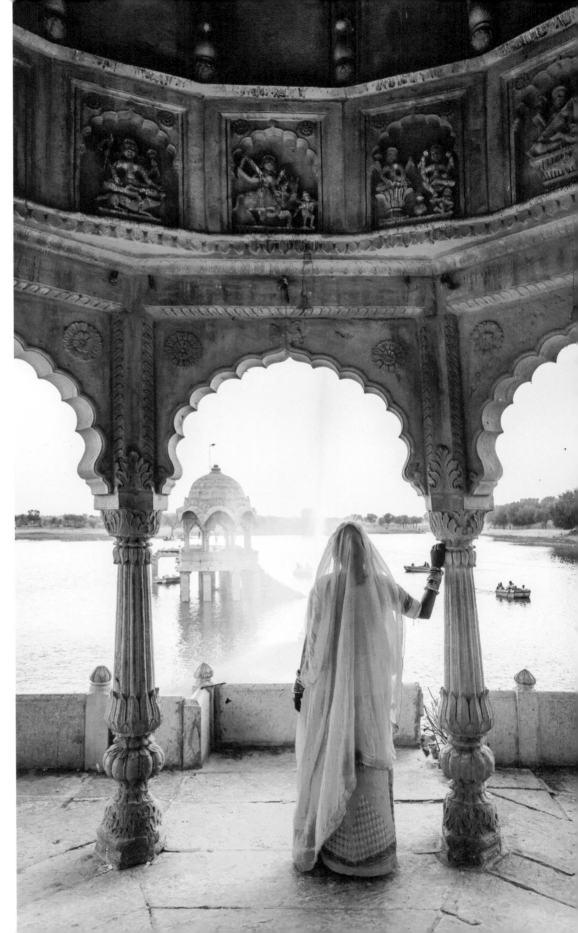

Above A monkey running along the walls of Jaipur's Amber Fort

Right A woman standing under an intricate pavilion on Gadi Sagar Lake in Jaisalmer

// DECEMBER

TORTOLA, BRITISH VIRGIN ISLANDS	**234**		HELSINKI AND LAPLAND, FINLAND	**244**
VIENNA, AUSTRIA	**236**		LAOS	**246**
KERALA, INDIA	**238**		SANTA FE, USA	**248**
CAYMAN ISLANDS, CARIBBEAN	**240**		EDINBURGH, SCOTLAND	**249**
SAN PEDRO DE ATACAMA, CHILE	**242**		SYDNEY, AUSTRALIA	**250**

Cockle pickers aboard
their boats on
Vembanad Lake, Kerala

TORTOLA

Caribbean British Virgin Islands
TORTOLA

WHY GO *Reliably sunny skies and balmy temperatures are hard to resist in December. Tortola possesses all the key ingredients for a relaxing winter getaway.*

Tortola is a place of repose, with beaches rivalling in beauty and solitude those of anywhere in the world. The island is scalloped by secluded coves and the north shore is fringed with endless stretches of champagne-coloured beaches: Brewers Bay, Cane Garden Bay, Elizabeth Beach and Long Bay are some of the loveliest.

Carefree and casual, Tortola has many great restaurants and bars that are perfect for lingering lunches and alfresco candlelit dinners. Dine on velvety crab callaloo and Johnny-cakes (a spicy okra stew with corn-bread) as you listen to the calming sounds of lapping waves. Later, head down to one of the many beach bars scattered around the bays and, with a potent rum cocktail in hand, dance the night away on the shore to the calypso music that throbs across the moonlit bay.

When you feel in need of some activity, take a trip to Road Town, Tortola's urban hub. The town is still steeped in its colonial past, with elegant wooden houses and an old-worldly feel. Stroll down the central shopping strip, narrow Main Street, and pick up some of the beautiful gold, emeralds and shells that Tortola is famed for, before taking the weight off your feet with a long lunch. If you're feeling adventurous, hire one of the power-boats bobbing alongside the jetties and explore the neighbouring islands that seem to float invitingly on the horizon. A sunset stroll along the sands is the perfect way to conclude the day.

When Else to Go
March–April The BVI Spring Regatta welcomes sailing boats for a week of sailing contests.

PLANNING YOUR TRIP **Getting there** International visitors can fly into San Juan (Puerto Rico) or Santo Domingo (Dominican Republic) and catch a connecting flight. **Getting around** There are plenty of taxis, or you can hire a car. Water taxis, ferries and small charter planes link Tortola to the other British Virgin Islands. **Weather** Tortola enjoys balmy weather with gentle, cooling trade winds. **Average temperature** 29°C / 84°F.

Waves lapping along
a palm-lined shore
on Tortola

VIENNA

Europe Austria
VIENNA

WHY GO *A visit over Christmas will give you a chance to enjoy the fabulous festive markets and dance the night away at the party in St Stephen's Square on New Year's Eve.*

Of all the cities in Europe, Vienna has the merriest Advent and Christmas imaginable, one that lasts for weeks and weeks, starting with the arrival of St Nicholas and his scary sidekick Krampus at the Christkindlmarkt.

Every year for centuries, Vienna has transformed into a winter wonderland with lights twinkling in the frosty nights and open-air Christmas markets popping up all over the city. These colourful markets sell a huge selection of beautifully made handicrafts, toys, decorations and tree ornaments, all carefully displayed. As you wander through the maze of stalls, the smell of roasted chestnuts, *Glühwein* (hot spiced wine), *Punsch* (fruit punch spiked with wine) and *Lebkuchen* (a moulded gingerbread) drifts through the air, tempting you to try the Christmas fare for which the Viennese markets are famed.

When it comes to tradition, Vienna pulls out all the stops – there are choirs that fill the city with song,

special marionette shows and an immense display of Nativity scenes. After a traditional Christmas, the party goes on. New Year's Eve in Vienna is one big celebration – a huge market extends along a mile-long strip linking the city's squares. The heart of the party is in the plaza around St Stephen's Cathedral, where revellers sip chilled champagne and dance into the night.

And there's more. New Year's Eve is merely a prelude to 300 balls that take place during January's Ball Season. There's nothing more quintessentially Viennese than a ball, so a waltz around the dance floor is the perfect end to your time in the city.

When Else to Go
September–October This is a great time to visit, as the summer crowds have gone, the air is crisp and clear, and there are plenty of cultural events, such as the Viennale Film Festival and the Long Night of Museums.

Above The Christkindl-markt, with its loaded stalls and festive lights, on Rathausplatz in front of Vienna's town hall

Right Glasses of warm *Glühwein*; decorated gingerbread on sale at the Christkindlmarkt; beautiful Christmas decorations twinkling in soft lighting

PLANNING YOUR TRIP **Getting there** International flights arrive into Vienna International Airport, 20 km (12 miles) southeast of the city. **Getting around** The best way to see Vienna is on foot. There is also a subway system (U-Bahn), as well as buses and trams. **Weather** December is cold, with some light snow. **Average temperature** 3°C / 37°F.

KERALA

Asia India
KERALA

WHY GO *It's during December that Kerala lives up to its nickname, "God's Own Country". The monsoon has ended, leaving a lush landscape in its wake. This is best seen by a journey through Kerala's backwaters.*

Still, green waters, channelled through rice paddies and dense coconut groves, only occasionally disturbed by the languid movement of a *kettuvallam* (rice barge): these are the palm-shaded lakes that make up Kerala's 900-km (560-mile) network of backwaters, a patchwork of land and water. Life here has remained distinctly rural, with locals living alongside animals and vegetable plots, worlds away from India's sprawling cities.

There is no more appropriate way to travel through these lush waterways than by *kettuvallam*, passing centuries-old fishing communities and abundant plantations at a leisurely pace. Originally used to ferry rice, these attractive wooden boats now meander through the waterways, shuttling children to and from school and delivering produce to local villages.

As the sun sets over the backwaters, silhouetting the palms against the sky, a deep peace settles, broken only by the occasional shriek of a monkey. This is an utterly enchanting experience, unlike anything else on the subcontinent.

When Else to Go
January–February The weather remains warm and dry.
August–September Boat races are held for the festival of Onam.

A traditional houseboat gliding along the beautiful palm-shaded backwaters of Kerala

PLANNING YOUR TRIP **Getting there** International flights arrive into Kochi and the state capital, Thiruvananthapuram. **Getting around** Use buses, trains or hire a driver (agree a fee first). You can only see the backwaters by boat. **Weather** It's balmy, with the monsoon finishing at the start of the month. **Average temperature** 30°C / 86°F.

A stingray swimming along the sandy sea floor, just beneath the water's surface, off the coast of Grand Cayman

CAYMAN
ISLANDS

Caribbean
CAYMAN ISLANDS

WHY GO *Warm waters, crystal-clear visibility and stunning marine life – December is the perfect time to visit these Caribbean islands for sensational scuba diving excursions.*

The cobalt-blue waters framing the Cayman Islands conceal a breath-taking underwater world studded with flashing shoals of brightly coloured fish, dazzling coral reef formations and eerie shipwrecks. This is a scuba diver's paradise. The dramatic, submerged landscape around the islands hosts more than 150 superb dive spots, each with its own distinct character, and catering to all levels of ability. There are night dives, day dives, wreck dives, cave dives: the choice is dizzying.

Avid divers shouldn't miss Cayman Brac, the farthest east of the three main islands and home to one of the Caribbean's most sensational dive spots. Here, the famed North Wall drops away to an astonishing 4,250 m (14,000 ft), while the steeper and more awesome South Wall drops away farther still, into the velvet blackness of the precipice below. The walls are alive with sponges, finger corals, sea fans and an incredible diversity of marine life, which includes moray eels, parrotfish, stingrays and green sea turtles. Less intrepid divers might prefer to opt for the excellent shallow dives nearby, which lead divers through caves and tunnels, and out across canyons and sublime towers of coral reef, where, on particularly clear days, the visibility can reach up to 46 m (150 ft). Dive into the blue and see for yourself.

When Else to Go
March Prices drop and the weather is lovely. **June** Swimmers race one mile as part of the Flowers Sea Swim.

PLANNING YOUR TRIP **Getting there** The international airport on Grand Cayman is the main arrival point. Little Cayman has daily inter-island flights. Cruise ships stop regularly. **Getting around** Hire cars, motorbikes and bicycles are available on Grand Cayman and Cayman Brac; bicycles and 4WD vehicles on Little Cayman. Taxis are plentiful. **Weather** Warm, clear skies and little rain. **Average temperature** 28°C / 82°F.

MARINE LIFE

The turquoise blue waters that surround the Cayman Islands support a dazzling array of marine life. Keep your eyes peeled for these aquatic critters.

Particularly plentiful in the waters around Grand Cayman, the multicoloured **parrotfish** *(above)*, with its beak-like mouth, helps to keep the coral clean and healthy while it feeds.

The **Caribbean reef shark** *(above)* is a fairly common sight in deeper channels of water near Little Cayman and Cayman Brac.

Diving and snorkelling are hugely popular on this island paradise. The ultimate reward? A rare sighting of an elusive **green sea turtle** *(above)* in the wild.

SAN PEDRO DE ATACAMA

An astronomer studying
the Milky Way in the
Atacama Desert

South America Chile
SAN PEDRO DE ATACAMA

WHY GO *Reach for the stars in northern Chile. December is the last month of spring, promising warm temperatures, fewer crowds and clear skies – the ideal conditions for stargazing in the desert.*

Shimmering salt flats and surreal rock formations, gushing geysers and emerald-green lakes, looming volcanoes and sheer-faced mountains, all watched over by stellar skies – welcome to San Pedro de Atacama, the driest desert on earth. Northern Chile's geography and lack of light pollution make this a truly heavenly place for stargazing. December is a glorious time to look up to San Pedro's night sky, glistening with stars, planets, constellations, nebulas, clusters and other celestial bodies. It's also quieter at this time of year, so you'll feel like you have the entire cosmos to yourself.

Stargazing tours provide an illuminating insight into the night sky, with astronomer-guides showing you how to read a "sky map" and pick out glittering stars, constellations and galaxies. Squint through telescopes to catch a glimpse of Jupiter, Saturn and its rings, and the Andromeda Galaxy, and use the specialist equipment provided to take your own incredible photos of the colossal cosmos stretching overhead.

A stargazing tour is best combined with a visit to the cutting-edge Atacama Large Millimeter Array (ALMA), the world's largest radio telescope. This remarkably powerful piece of technology allows astronomers to study the origins of the universe and the formation of the first galaxies. To us mere mortals, it's a mind-expanding experience; outer space will never feel so close at hand.

When Else to Go

June The lively Fiesta de San Pedro y San Pablo (Feast of Saint Peter and Saint Paul) takes place on 29 June, with music, dancing, parades and lots of food and drink.

PLANNING YOUR TRIP **Getting there** The nearest airport – El Loa – is in the city of Calama, 100 km (62 miles) northwest of San Pedro. Regular buses run from El Loa to San Pedro. **Getting around** You can walk, cycle, take a taxi or hire a car to visit some nearby sights, but organized tours are the best way to explore the region. **Weather** Warm with occasional light showers. **Average temperature** 24°C / 75°F.

"This is a world of glistening white, broken only by the intensely vivid colours of woolly winter hats."

Left Reindeer walking through the snowy landscape of Lemmenjoki National Park, Lapland

Above A cosy campfire in Lapland; snow-topped trees and a cute cabin

LAPLAND

HELSINKI

Europe Finland
HELSINKI AND LAPLAND

WHY GO *No one does Christmas like the Finns. Visitors to the capital, Helsinki, will find festive cheer at every turn. Continue on to Lapland for sugar-coated, childish jollity – this is, after all, the home of Santa Claus.*

The Finns love winter and the trappings of Christmas that come hand-in-hand with the season. They revel in it and invite the world to join them on frozen ponds and ski slopes. It's so cold that sometimes the sea even freezes over and brave locals don their ice skates. This is a world of glistening white, broken only by the intensely vivid colours of woolly winter hats, scarves and mittens.

The best place to start a festive Finnish foray is in the capital, Helsinki, a city that has both the style of its Nordic neighbours and the romance of Eastern Europe. Here you'll discover glittering fairy lights, magical markets, Christmas carols and festive shows galore.

But you can't come all this way and not visit Santa in Finnish Lapland. By early December, holiday sights, sounds and aromas fill the land: the excited squeal of children catching a glimpse of Santa, sausages and herring sizzling over glowing coals, the aroma of freshly baked honey cakes as you enter a café, mellow brass notes from a street musician's horn and the hubbub of open-air markets filled with shoppers. At least one booth will have a steaming cauldron of *glögi*, a mouth-tingling brew of red wine, spices, raisins and blackcurrant juice that warms you to your toes. This really is a winter wonderland for little and big kids alike.

When Else to Go
February Lapland is buried in snow and the magical Northern Lights often make an appearance. **September** The trees shed their foliage in Helsinki, known locally as *"ruska"*.

PLANNING YOUR TRIP **Getting there** Flights arrive into Helsinki Airport, 20 km (12 miles) from the city centre. **Getting around** Buses, trams, trains and boats offer comprehensive transport in Helsinki. Lapland is 830 km (515 miles) north and can be reached by an 11-hour train ride or a domestic flight. **Weather** Cold with frequent light snow. **Average temperature** -2°C / 28°F.

LAOS

Asia
LAOS

WHY GO *December's clear and bright skies provide the perfect backdrop for seeing the sights of Laos while travelling down the fast-flowing Mekong.*

Situated high in the mist-shrouded mountains of northern Laos, Luang Prabang, once the royal capital, sits on a promontory on the broad Mekong River. It remains a treasure trove of ornately carved wooden temples, covered with golden stencils and shimmering mosaics, with cascading multi-tiered roofs.

There is no better way to arrive in Luang Prabang than by boat on the Mekong, a memorable journey that starts at the Thai border. Sailing down its swirling waters, past sheer limestone cliffs and jungle-clad mountains, unspoiled land-scapes, picturesque villages and sacred caves come into view.

Continue down the river to Vientiane, Laos's laid-back capital. The peace here is broken by tuk-tuks rattling along to the morning market where visitors bargain for dazzling raw silk and silver jewellery. In the evening, watch the spectacular sunset turn the Mekong from red to gold and reflect on this little-changed land.

When Else to Go
April Boun Pi Mai (Lao New Year) is celebrated across three days, with ceremonies, parades, boat races and lots of water.

PLANNING YOUR TRIP **Getting there** Fly to Thailand's Chiang Mai International Airport and travel to Chiang Khong to cross the border into Laos. Take a bus to Huay Xai (marked Bokeo) and head to the pier to board your boat. **Getting around** The stops en route are best explored on foot. **Weather** Dry and hot. **Average temperature** 30°C / 86°F.

Clockwise from top left
Riverboat on the Mekong at sunset; money offerings outside a Buddhist temple in Vientiane; young Buddhist monks walking by Wat Siphoutabath, Luang Prabang

North America USA
SANTA FE

SANTA FE

WHY GO *Christmas celebrations occur throughout the month, but don't miss the dazzlingly unique Santa Fe festivities from 23 to 26 December.*

It's a simple thing really, a candle, in a paper bag, filled with sand. Light the candle at dusk and the little lantern, known as a *farolito*, glows with a warm, inviting light. Now imagine the tens of thousands that line the city's roads and windowsills of the buildings.

Christmas in Santa Fe is, of course, more than *farolitos*. It's the traditions that reach back hundreds of years and celebrate Santa Fe's powerful and captivating blend of Native American, Spanish and Anglo cultures. It's the cold, clear nights where the air seems so transparent that you can see forever, and the starlit night sky dazzles from horizon to horizon like an inverted bowl of celestial fairy lights. In the *pueblos* (Native American villages) that surround Santa Fe, Christmas is a special time. Here, ceremonies blend Christian practice with tribal traditions. Their echoes are the ancient hymn of this startling land that lies on the high plateaus between snow-covered mountains and the endless western desert.

When Else to Go
September Mild temperatures and plenty of festivities, including the Fiesta de Santa Fe.

PLANNING YOUR TRIP **Getting there** International flights arrive into Albuquerque, New Mexico, 105 km (65 miles) from Santa Fe. **Getting around** The city is best explored on foot; hire a car if you want to go further afield. **Weather** Sunny and dry. **Average temperature** 7°C / 46°F.

The buildings on Santa Fe Plaza, illuminated by tiny *farolitos*, twinkling in the night

The Torchlight Procession marches down the Royal Mile to mark the start of Edinburgh's Hogmanay

EDINBURGH

Europe Scotland
EDINBURGH

WHY GO *Nights grow darker and colder towards the end of the year, so wrap up warm for a truly memorable party at Edinburgh's Hogmanay.*

At the craggy base of Castle Rock crowds swell to watch fireworks arc overhead and dazzling rockets rain down through the whisky-tinged air. Edinburgh is known for many things but, above all, it's known for Hogmanay, its annual end-of-year, zeitgeist-defining party. This hedonistic three-day curtain raiser to the New Year brings in some 150,000 revellers, all of whom become increasingly animated as the week draws to its climax – midnight on 31 December. There's plenty to occupy you during the build-up: concerts, whisky tastings, bands, DJs, Highland dances and the Torchlight Procession from the castle to Holyrood Park. It's the greatest New Year celebration on earth, so why not join the party?

When Else to Go
August The Edinburgh Festival Fringe – the largest arts festival in the world – comes to town.

PLANNING YOUR TRIP **Getting there** Edinburgh International Airport has bus and tram links to the city. **Getting around** Buses are reliable, but it is easy to get around on foot. **Weather** Cold, wet and windy. **Average temperature** 3°C / 37°F.

SYDNEY

Oceania Australia
SYDNEY

WHY GO *Australia's "Harbour City" is the country's party capital and New Year is the biggest celebration of all. Head to the glittering waterfront to witness the world's most famous fireworks display.*

Sydney is a handsome city set around a sparkling harbour and graced by the impressive Sydney Harbour Bridge. Perhaps most famous is the Opera House, its multi-peaked roof evocative of a ship in full sail. A cultural and postmodern metropolis, Sydney has become one of the best places to enjoy New Year's Eve, when the city's waterfront is transformed into a dazzling set piece.

As the light slowly fades on the big day, the harbour fills with twinkling, bobbing boats. Then, at midnight, fireworks erupt from the bridge and light up the sky with eyeball-searing intensity. A curtain of liquid fire drops from the bridge to the water, while volleys of rockets release layer-upon-layer of coloured sheets of flame, a psychedelic starburst of colour. When it finishes, it's as though someone has turned the lights out, and the spectators go

wild. There's no more Aussie way to celebrate than with a barbecue and a few "tinnies" (cans of beer) at one of the viewpoints. The parties go on till dawn – and beyond.

On New Year's Day, head down to Bondi Beach for a dip in the sea – the perfect remedy for a sore head. If you feel up to it, join locals straddling their surf boards and waiting for the perfect tide. Each big wave's arrival is signalled by a burst of frantic activity, with the successful riding the water into shore. Embrace the brine and start the new year the Aussie way.

When Else to Go
January Events during this month include the Big Bash cricket league, and three weeks of arts and culture events for the Sydney Festival.
October The final of the Rugby League, a huge event in the city's calendar.

PLANNING YOUR TRIP **Getting there** Flights arrive into Sydney Airport, 12 km (7 miles) from the city centre. **Getting around** The city has an excellent network of buses, light rail, metro and ferries. Taxis are also cheap. **Weather** Warm weather is virtually guaranteed in December, with cooling sea breezes on the waterfront. **Average temperature** 24°C / 75°F.

Dazzling fireworks exploding over the iconic roof of Sydney Opera House

INDEX

A

Activity holidays
  Bahamas 228–9
  Borneo (Indonesia) 188–9
  Corsica (France) 148–9
  Kilimanjaro (Tanzania)
    16–17
  Pembrokeshire (Wales)
    144–7
  Queensland (Australia)
    204–5
  Queenstown (New
    Zealand) 192
Agra (India) 30–31
Aitutaki (Cook Islands)
  224–5
Albuquerque (USA) 206–7
Amalfi Coast (Italy) 92–3
Angkor Wat (Cambodia)
  38–9
Antarctica 46–7
Antigua (Guatemala) 68–9
Argentina
  Buenos Aires 196–7
  Patagonia 18–19
Athens (Greece) 90–91
Aurora borealis
  Tromsø (Norway) 22–3
Australia
  Ningaloo 54–5
  Queensland 204–5
  Sydney 250–51
  Tasmania 226–7
  Uluru 124–5
Austria
  Salzburg 143
  Vienna 236–7

B

Bahamas 228–9
Bali (Indonesia) 104–5
Bangkok (Thailand) 24
Barcelona (Spain) 118–19
Barsana (India) 52–3

Beaches
  Aitutaki (Cook Islands)
    224–5
  Bahamas 228–9
  Jamaica 25
  Maldives (Indian Ocean)
    20–21
  Miami (USA) 48
  Mu Ko Ang Thong
    National Park (Thailand)
    40–41
  Perhentian Islands
    (Malaysia) 89
  Queensland (Australia)
    204–5
  San Sebastián (Spain)
    60–61
  Sydney (Australia)
    250–51
  Tortola (British Virgin
    Islands) 234–5
Beijing (China) 190–91
Berlin (Germany) 150–51
Black Forest (Germany) 163
Bolivia
  La Paz 101
Bollenstreek (Netherlands)
  78–9
Borneo (Indonesia)
  188–9
Borobudur (Indonesia)
  160–61
Boston (USA) 94–5
Brazil
  Iguaçu Falls 82–3
  Rio de Janeiro 49
Britain *see* England;
  Scotland; Wales
British Virgin Islands
  Tortola 234–5
Budapest (Hungary) 202
Buenos Aires (Argentina)
  196–7
Burgundy (France) 220

C

California Coast (USA)
  208–9
Cambodia
  Angkor Wat 38–9

Camping
  Himalayas (Nepal) 56
  North Island (New
    Zealand) 42–3
Canada
  Coast to Coast 128–9
  Montreal 122
  Ottawa 34–5
  Whistler 57
Caribbean
  Bahamas 228–9
  Cayman Islands 240–41
  Tortola (British Virgin
    Islands) 234–5
Cayman Islands 240–41
Chicago (USA) 62–3
Chile
  Patagonia 18–19
  San Pedro de Atacama
    242–3
China
  Beijing 190–91
  Silk Road 112–13
  Yunnan 120–21
Churches *see* Religious
  interest
City breaks
  Athens (Greece) 90–91
  Bangkok (Thailand) 24
  Barcelona (Spain) 118–19
  Beijing (China) 190–91
  Berlin (Germany) 150–51
  Boston (USA) 94–5
  Budapest (Hungary) 202
  Buenos Aires (Argentina)
    196–7
  Chicago (USA) 62–3
  Copenhagen (Denmark)
    156–7
  Edinburgh (Scotland) 249
  Havana (Cuba) 32
  Helsinki (Finland) 244–5
  Istanbul (Turkey) 84–7
  Kyoto (Japan) 80–81
  La Paz (Bolivia) 101
  London (England) 186–7
  Lucerne (Switzerland) 162
  Marrakech (Morocco)
    64–5
  Miami (USA) 48
  Montreal (Canada) 122
  Munich (Germany) 178

City breaks (cont.)
  New York City (USA)
    114–15
  Prague (Czech Republic)
    100
  Rio de Janeiro (Brazil) 49
  Rome (Italy) 132–3
  Salzburg (Austria) 143
  San Sebastián (Spain) 60–61
  Seoul (South Korea) 222–3
  St Petersburg (Russia) 10–11
  Sydney (Australia) 250–51
  Tokyo (Japan) 218–19
  Valencia (Spain) 58–9
  Vienna (Austria) 236–7
  Washington, DC (USA) 142
  Zermatt (Switzerland) 36–7
Coast to Coast (Canada)
  128–9
Coastlines
  Amalfi Coast (Italy) 92–3
  California Coast (USA)
    208–9
  Dalmatian Coast (Croatia)
    134–5
  Fjord cruise (Norway)
    72–3
  Lycian Coast (Turkey)
    184–5
  Mozambique 174–5
  Ningaloo (Australia) 54–5
  Pembrokeshire (Wales)
    144–7
  Queensland (Australia)
    204–5
  West Coast (Scotland)
    106–7
  see also Beaches; Islands
Colorado Plateau (USA)
  108–9
Cook Islands
  Aitutaki 224–5
Copenhagen (Denmark)
  156–7
Corsica (France) 148–9
Costa Rica 26–7
Crete (Greece) 110–11
Croatia
  Dalmatian Coast 134–5
Cruises
  Burgundy (France) 220
  Fjord cruise (Norway) 72–3

Cruises (cont.)
　Kerala (India) 238–9
　Laos 246–7
　Lycian Coast (Turkey)
　　184–5
　Mississippi cruise (USA)
　　221
　Patagonia (Chile and
　　Argentina) 18–19
Cuba
　Havana 32–3
Cultural interests
　Prague (Czech Republic)
　　100
　Salzburg (Austria) 143
　St Petersburg (Russia) 11
Czech Republic
　Prague 100

D

Dalmatian Coast (Croatia)
　134–5
Denmark
　Copenhagen 156–7
Diving and snorkelling
　Aitutaki (Cook Islands)
　　224–5
　Cayman Islands 240–41
　Galápagos Islands (Ecuador)
　　88
　Mozambique 174–5
　Mu Ko Ang Thong
　　National Park (Thailand)
　　40–41
　Ningaloo (Australia) 54–5
　Perhentian Islands
　　(Malaysia) 89
　Queensland (Australia)
　　204–5
Driving
　Amalfi Coast (Italy)
　　92–3
　California Coast (USA)
　　208–9
　Crete (Greece) 110–11
　Dalmatian Coast (Croatia)
　　134–5
　Iceland 126–7
　Kruger National Park
　　(South Africa) 136–7

Driving (cont.)
　North Island (New
　　Zealand) 42–3
　Provence (France) 154–5
　West Coast (Scotland)
　　106–7

E

Ecuador
　Galápagos Islands 88
Edinburgh (Scotland) 249
Ella (Sri Lanka) 170–71
England
　Lake District 98–9
　London 186–7
Ethiopia
　Lalibela 12–13

F

Festivals and events
　Albuquerque (USA) 206–7
　Antigua (Guatemala) 68–9
　Athens (Greece) 90–91
　Barcelona (Spain) 118–19
　Barsana (India) 52–3
　Berlin (Germany) 150–51
　Chicago (USA) 62–3
　Edinburgh (Scotland) 249
　Galway (Ireland) 179
　Helsinki and Lapland
　　(Finland) 244–5
　Mongolia 140–41
　Montreal (Canada) 122
　Munich (Germany) 178
　Oaxaca (Mexico) 210–11
　Ottawa (Canada) 34–5
　Rio de Janeiro (Brazil) 49
　Rome (Italy) 132–3
　Santa Fe (USA) 248
　Sydney (Australia) 250–51
　Tennessee (USA) 123
　Valencia (Spain) 58–9
　Vermont (USA) 182–3
　Washington, DC (USA) 142
　West Coast (Scotland) 106–7
Finland
　Helsinki and Lapland 244–5
Fjord cruise (Norway) 72–3

Flowers
　Bollenstreek (Netherlands)
　　78–9
　Kyoto (Japan) 80–81
　Provence (France) 154–5
Food and drink
　Burgundy (France) 220
　Loire Valley (France) 203
　San Sebastián (Spain) 60–61
　Seoul (South Korea) 222–3
　Tortola (British Virgin
　　Islands) 234–5
　Tuscany (Italy) 198–201
Forests
　Black Forest (Germany) 163
　Vermont (USA) 182–3
France
　Burgundy 220
　Corsica 148–9
　Loire Valley 203
　Provence 154–5

G

Galápagos Islands
　(Ecuador) 88
Galway (Ireland) 179
Germany
　Berlin 150–51
　Black Forest 163
　Munich 178
Glacier Bay National Park
　(USA) 168–9
Greece
　Athens 90–91
　Crete 110–11
Guatemala
　Antigua 68–9

H

Havana (Cuba) 32–3
Hawai'i
　Kaua'i (USA) 212–13
Helsinki (Finland) 244–5
Hiking and trekking
　Black Forest (Germany) 163
　Colorado Plateau (USA)
　　108–9
　Crete (Greece) 110–11

Hiking and trekking (cont.)
　Himalayas (Nepal) 56
　Kilimanjaro (Tanzania)
　　16–17
　Lake District (England)
　　98–9
　Machu Picchu (Peru)
　　130–31
　Manu National Park (Peru)
　　164–5
　Mu Ko Ang Thong
　　National Park (Thailand)
　　40–41
　Pembrokeshire (Wales)
　　144–7
　Seoul (South Korea) 222–3
　Slovenia 172–3
　Tasmania (Australia) 226–7
　Yellowstone National Park
　　(USA) 166–7
　Yunnan (China) 120–21
Himalayas (Nepal) 56
Historic buildings
　Agra (India) 30–31
　Angkor Wat (Cambodia)
　　38–9
　Athens (Greece) 90–91
　Borobudur (Indonesia)
　　160–61
　Laos 246–7
　Loire Valley (France) 203
　Petra (Jordan) 74–5
　Samarkand (Uzbekistan)
　　76–7
　Silk Road (China) 112–13
　St Petersburg (Russia) 11
　Yucatán (Mexico) 66–7
Hungary
　Budapest 202

I

Iceland 126–7
Iguaçu Falls (Brazil) 82–3
India
　Agra 30–31
　Barsana 52–3
　Kerala 238–9
　Rajasthan 230–31
Indian Ocean
　Maldives 20–21

Indonesia
  Bali 104–5
  Borneo 188–9
  Borobudur 160–61
Ireland
  Galway 179
Islands
  Aitutaki (Cook Islands) 224–5
  Bahamas 228–9
  Bali (Indonesia) 104–5
  Cayman Islands 240–41
  Corsica (France) 148–9
  Crete (Greece) 110–11
  Dalmatian Coast (Croatia) 134–5
  Galápagos Islands (Ecuador) 88
  Havana (Cuba) 32
  Iceland 126–7
  Jamaica 25
  Kaua'i (Hawai'i, USA) 212–13
  Madeira (Portugal) 193
  Maldives (Indian Ocean) 20–21
  Mu Ko Ang Thong National Park (Thailand) 40–41
  Perhentian Islands (Malaysia) 89
  Svalbard (Norway) 152–3
  Tortola (British Virgin Islands) 234–5
Istanbul (Turkey) 84–7
Italy
  Amalfi Coast 92–3
  Rome 132–3
  Tuscany 198–201

J

Jackson Hole (USA) 14–15
Jamaica 25
Japan
  Kyoto 80–81
  Tokyo 218–19
Jordan
  Petra 74–5
Jungles
  Borneo (Indonesia) 188–9

Jungles (cont.)
  Costa Rica 26–7
  Manu National Park (Peru) 164–5
  Queensland (Australia) 204–5
  Uganda 44–5

K

Kandy (Sri Lanka) 170–71
Kaua'i (Hawai'i, USA) 212–13
Kerala (India) 238–9
Kilimanjaro (Tanzania) 16–17
Korea see South Korea
Kruger National Park (South Africa) 136–7
Kyoto (Japan) 80–81

L

Lakes
  Kerala (India) 238–9
  Lake District (England) 98–9
  Lucerne (Switzerland) 162
  Slovenia 172–3
Lalibela (Ethiopia) 12–13
Laos 246–7
La Paz (Bolivia) 101
Lapland (Finland) 244–5
Loire Valley (France) 203
London (England) 186–7
Lucerne (Switzerland) 162
Lycian Coast (Turkey) 184–5

M

Machu Picchu (Peru) 130–31
Madeira (Portugal) 193
Magellan, Strait of (Patagonia) 18
Malaysia
  Perhentian Islands 89
Maldives (Indian Ocean) 20–21
Manu National Park (Peru) 164–5
Marrakech (Morocco) 64–5

Mexico
  Oaxaca 210–11
  Yucatán 66–7
Miami (USA) 48
Mississippi cruise (USA) 221
Mongolia 140–41
Montreal (Canada) 122
Morocco
  Marrakech 64–5
Mountains
  Himalayas (Nepal) 56
  Kilimanjaro (Tanzania) 16–17
  Lake District (England) 98–9
  Machu Picchu (Peru) 130–31
  Whistler (Canada) 57
  Zermatt (Switzerland) 36–7
Mozambique 174–5
Mu Ko Ang Thong National Park (Thailand) 40–41
Munich (Germany) 178

N

Namib-Naukluft Park (Namibia) 180–81
National parks
  Glacier Bay (USA) 168–9
  Kruger (South Africa) 136–7
  Manu (Peru) 164–5
  Mu Ko Ang Thong (Thailand) 40–41
  Yellowstone (USA) 166–7
Natural wonders
  Colorado Plateau (USA) 108–9
  Fjord cruise (Norway) 72–3
  Glacier Bay National Park (USA) 168–9
  Himalayas (Nepal) 56
  Iceland 126–7
  Iguaçu Falls (Brazil) 82–3
  Kaua'i (Hawai'i, USA) 212–13
  Lake District (England) 98–9
  Namib-Naukluft Park (Namibia) 180–81
  Northern Lights (Norway) 22–3

Natural wonders (cont.)
  North Island (New Zealand) 42–3
  San Pedro de Atacama (Chile) 242–3
  Uluru (Australia) 124–5
  Vermont (USA) 182–3
  Victoria Falls (Zambia and Zimbabwe) 102
  Yellowstone National Park (USA) 166–7
  Yunnan (China) 120–21
Nepal
  Himalayas 56
Netherlands
  Bollenstreek 78–9
New York City (USA) 114–15
New Zealand
  North Island 42–3
  Queenstown 192
Nightlife
  Havana (Cuba) 32
  see also Festivals and events
Ningaloo (Australia) 54–5
Northern Lights (Norway) 22–3
North Island (New Zealand) 42–3
Norway
  Fjord cruise 72–3
  Svalbard 152–3
  Tromsø 22–3

O

Oaxaca (Mexico) 210–11
Ottawa (Canada) 34–5

P

Pampering
  Bali (Indonesia) 104–5
  Budapest (Hungary) 202
Patagonia (Chile and Argentina) 18–19
Pembrokeshire (Wales) 144–7
Perhentian Islands (Malaysia) 89
Peru
  Machu Picchu 130–31
  Manu National Park 164–5

Petra (Jordan) 74–5
Polar regions
  Antarctica 46–7
  Svalbard (Norway) 152–3
  Tromsø (Norway) 22–3
Portugal
  Madeira 193
Prague (Czech Republic)
  100
Provence (France) 154–5

Q

Queensland (Australia)
  204–5
Queenstown (New Zealand)
  192

R

Rail journeys
  Coast to Coast (Canada)
    128–9
  Kandy to Ella (Sri Lanka)
    170–71
  Rajasthan (India) 230–31
  Silk Road (China) 112–13
Rainforests see Jungles
Rajasthan (India) 230–31
Religious interest
  Angkor Wat (Cambodia)
    38–9
  Antigua (Guatemala) 68–9
  Borobudur (Indonesia)
    160–61
  Lalibela (Ethiopia) 12–13
  Laos 246–7
  Yucatán (Mexico) 66–7
Rio de Janeiro (Brazil) 49
Rivers
  Laos 246–7
  Loire Valley (France) 203
  Manu National Park (Peru)
    164–5
  Mississippi cruise (USA)
    221
  Yunnan (China) 120–21
Rome (Italy) 132–3
Russia
  St Petersburg 10–11

S

Salzburg (Austria) 143
Samarkand (Uzbekistan) 76–7
San Pedro de Atacama (Chile)
  242–3
San Sebastián (Spain) 60–61
Santa Fe (USA) 248
Scotland
  Edinburgh 249
  West Coast 106–7
Seoul (South Korea) 222–3
Silk Road (China) 112–13
Skiing see Winter sports
Slovenia 172–3
Snorkelling see Diving and
  snorkelling
South Africa
  Kruger National Park 136–7
South Korea
  Seoul 222–3
Spain
  Barcelona 118–19
  San Sebastián 60–61
  Valencia 58–9
Sri Lanka
  Kandy to Ella 170–71
Stargazing
  San Pedro de Atacama
    (Chile) 242–3
St Petersburg (Russia) 10–11
Svalbard (Norway) 152–3
Switzerland
  Lucerne 162
  Zermatt 36–7
Sydney (Australia) 250–51

T

Tanzania
  Kilimanjaro 16–17
Tasmania (Australia)
  226–7
Tennessee (USA) 123
Thailand
  Bangkok 24
  Mu Ko Ang Thong
    National Park 40–41
Tokyo (Japan) 218–19
Tortola (Britain Virgin
  Islands) 234–5
Trekking see Hiking and
  trekking
Tromsø (Norway) 22–3
Turkey
  Istanbul 84–7
  Lycian Coast 184–5
Tuscany (Italy) 198–201

U

Uganda 44–5
Uluru (Australia) 124–5
United States of America
  Albuquerque 206–7
  Boston 94–5
  California Coast 208–9
  Chicago 62–3
  Colorado Plateau 108–9
  Glacier Bay National Park
    168–9
  Jackson Hole 14–15
  Kaua'i (Hawai'i) 212–13
  Miami 48
  Mississippi cruise 221
  New York City 114–15
  Northeast Vermont 182–3
  Santa Fe 248
  Tennessee 123
  Washington, DC 142
  Yellowstone National Park
    166–7
Uzbekistan
  Samarkand 76–7

V

Valencia (Spain) 58–9
Vermont (USA) 182–3
Victoria Falls (Zambia and
  Zimbabwe) 102
Vienna (Austria) 236–7
Vietnam 216–17
Virgin Islands (British)
  Tortola 234–5

W

Wales
  Pembrokeshire 144–7
Washington, DC 142
Waterfalls
  Iguaçu Falls 82–3
  Victoria Falls (Zambia and
    Zimbabwe) 102
Water sports
  Sydney (Australia) 250–51
  see also Diving and
    snorkelling
West Coast (Scotland) 106–7
Whistler (Canada) 57
Wildlife
  Aitutaki (Cook Islands) 224–5
  Antarctica 46–7
  Borneo (Indonesia) 188–9
  Cayman Islands 240–41
  Costa Rica 26–7
  Galápagos Islands
    (Ecuador) 88
  Glacier Bay National Park
    (USA) 168–9
  Kruger National Park
    (South Africa) 136–7
  Manu National Park (Peru)
    164–5
  Namib-Naukluft Park
    (Namibia) 180–81
  Ningaloo (Australia) 54–5
  Patagonia (Chile and
    Argentina) 18–19
  Svalbard (Norway) 152–3
  Uganda 44–5
Winter sports
  Jackson Hole (USA) 14–15
  Whistler (Canada) 57
  Zermatt (Switzerland) 36–7

Y

Yellowstone National Park
  (USA) 166–7
Yucatán (Mexico) 66–7
Yunnan (China) 120–21

Z

Zambia
  Victoria Falls 102
Zermatt (Switzerland) 36–7
Zimbabwe

ACKNOWLEDGMENTS

The publisher would like to thank the following for their contributions (in alphabetical order): J.P. Anderson, David Atkinson, Christopher Baker, Pam Barrett, Eleanor Berman, Shawn Blore, Philip Briggs, Christopher Catling, Sue Dobson, Mary Fitzpatrick, Rebecca Ford, Paul Franklin, Aruna Ghose, Jeremy Gray, Paul Greenberg, Eric Grossman, Graeme Harwood, Denise Heywood, Andrew Humphreys, Nick Inman, Yvonne Jeffery, Evelyn Kanter, Christopher Knowles, Tania Kollias, Simon Lewis, Frances Linzee Gordon, Rachel Lovelock, Sinead McGovern, Jenny McKelvie, Robin McKelvie, Mari Nicholson, John Noble, Georgina Palffy, Laura Byrne Paquet, Don Philpott, Eleanor Radford, Nick Rider, Barbara Rodgers, Andrew Sanger, Juergen Scheunemann, Deanna Swaney, Hugh Taylor, Samantha Tidy, Craig Turp, Ross Velton, Joanna Williams, Roger Williams, Helena Zukowski

PICTURE CREDITS

The publisher would like to thank the following for their kind permission to reproduce their photographs:

Key: a-above; b-below/bottom; c-centre; f-far; l-left; r-right; t-top

4Corners: Jordan Banks 162–3; Marco Gaiotti 45bc; Susanne Kremer 154–5, 187bc, 220–21b; Arcangelo Piai 186–7t; Maurizio Rellini 231r; Reinhard Schmid 178b; Anna Serrano 236–7t; Richard Taylor 179t; Francesco Tremolada 36–7.

Alamy Stock Photo: age fotostock 118bc, / Antonio Gravante 93cla; Arco Images GmbH / Arco / F. Schneider 41fcra; Mark Bassett 99br; Paul Brown 74crb; Cavan / Gabe Rogel 15bl; Cosmo Condina 122b; EggImages 185cra; Philip Game 19crb; Jane Gould 41cr; Stephen Harrison 34br; Hemis / Gil Giuglio 225cra, / Escudero Patrick 203l; Justin Hofman 46–7; Bob Hurley 34bl; imageBROKER / Olaf Krüger 232–3, / Moritz Wolf 64clb; Jon Arnold Images Ltd / Michele Falzone 93cl; Scott Kemper 182–3t; Muslianshah Masrie 53tr; mauritius images GmbH / ClickAlps 22cr, / Per-Andre Hoffmann 140–41, / Frank Lukasseck 113tr, / New Zealand Māori Arts and Crafts Institute at Te Puia, Rotorua / Michael Runkel 84br, / Gerhard Wild 237br; Rose-Marie Murray 221tr; National Geographic Image Collection 164–5t, 174–5b, / Chris Bickford 241crb, / Cesare Naldi 22cra; nekphotos 53tc;

Sergi Reboredo 225fcra; robertharding / Kimberly Walker 14; Stocktrek Images, Inc. / Brook Peterson 241crc; Jeremy Sutton-Hibbert 107clb; Nicholas Tinelli 74cra; WaterFrame 175tc; Andrew Wilson 248–9; Jan Wlodarczyk 113br, 192–3; Xinhua / Lu Zhe 85br; ZUMA Press, Inc. 118br.

AWL Images: Peter Adams 171tr; Jon Arnold 24t, 32cr, 32br, 82–3; Aurora Photos 246–7b; Walter Bibikow 247tc; Marco Bottigelli 132–3; Demetrio Carrasco 197bl; Matteo Colombo 112cr; Nigel Pavitt 13tl, 39bc; Doug Pearson 24–5b; Mattes Rene 217bl.

Depositphotos Inc: Baranov_Evgenii 202b.

Dreamstime.com: Andersastphoto 149cr; BarbaraCerovsek 173cr; Jakub Barzycki 40; Lukas Bischoff 196; Thomas Brissiaud 34–5t; Aurora Esperanza Ángeles Flores 130fcra; Markus Gann 43; Georgiakari 78; Helen Hotson 106–7; Tom Meaker 149crb; Glenn Nagel 248b; Cj Nattanai 223br; Sean Pavone 214–15; Peek Creative Collective 101b; Matthew Ragen 74cr; Rosshelen 61br; Alexander Shalamov 175tl; Igor Stevanovic 173cra; Tenkende 93bl; Matthew Train 144–5; Martin Valigursky 225crb.

Getty Images: 500px / Mikeal Beland 158–9, / Lukas Huber 64cl, / Daniel Kay 98, / Anton Komlev 244cr, / Yash Sheth 52–3b, / Ravi Valdiya 73tc; AFP / Cris Bouroncle 130cra, / Tobias Schwarz 151clb; Steve Allen 225fcr; Arctic-Images 26–7t; artherng 38–9t; Sirachai Arunrugstichai 41fcr; Aurora Photos / Carl D. Walsh 183bc; Adél Békefi 91bl; Walter Bibikow 95t, 234–5; Paul Biris 39bl; Levente Bodo 138–9; Kitti Boonnitrod 16; Boston Red Sox / Billie Weiss 95bl, 95br; Malcolm P Chapman 219br; Matteo Colombo 60–61, 224–5b; coolbiere photograph 222; Corbis / Jeff Vanuga 153tl; Cultura RM Exclusive / Philip Lee Harvey 244clb; Ian Cumming 58cla, 58r; David Merron Photography 152br; Jeff Diener 27cb; distant lands 12br; Ruben Earth 18–19b; Neil Emmerson 65br; Enn Li Photography 183br; EyeEm / Roberto Anania 33, / Cristian Bortes 79bl, / Tom Eversley 107cla, / Till Findl 22br, / Addy Ho 167bc, / Daniel Klatzer 172, / Erlend Krumsvik 73tr, / Scott Puetz 206cr, / Shawn Walters 166–7t; Grant Faint 204–5; Brit Finucci 136–7; fitopardo.com 211clb; National Geographic Image Collection / Chris Schmid 44–5t, / Ralph Lee Hopkins

153r; Geraint Rowland Photography 211cla; Marc Guitard 13r; Zsolt Hlinka 70–71; Bjorn Holland 76cr; Jeff Hunter 241cra; JKboy Jatenipat 18–19t; John Crux Photography 170–71b, 188bl; Wolfgang Kaehler 108br; Dave G Kelly 64cla; Katja Kreder 76bl; Jonathan Lewis 145br; Vincenzo Lombardo 10bl; David Madison 168–9; Philippe Marion 68br; Matt Anderson Photography 166–7b; Cormac McCreesh 175tr; Buda Mendes 49t; Moment / Luis Dafos 247tr, / Nadya Kulagina 240, / Naomi Rahim 244tr; James Morgan 188–9t; Nature Picture Library / Anup Shah 188bc; Nick Brundle Photography 125br; Ed Norton 88–9; Jake Norton 56bl; Jose Oliveira 6cl; Scott Olson 62–3; PEC Photo 200–201; Juan Pelegrín 6tl; Peter Zelei Images 194–5; Anton Petrus 86–7; Ph. Francesco Ciccotti 176–7; Pixelchrome Inc 76tr; Ratnakorn Piyasirisorost 75; Adrian Pope 30–31; Joe Daniel Price 6b, 96–7, 146–7; Joe Regan 128–9b; robertharding / Oliver Wintzen 69; Michael Roberts 145bl; SammyVision 54–5; Shestock 104br; shomos uddin 64–5; Simon Phelps Photography 180–81; SinghaphanAllB 28–9, 102–3; SOPA Images / LightRocket 151br; Kyle Sparks 192b; Alexander Spatari 114–15; SPC#JAYJAY 100–101; Inti St Clair 217br; Stocktrek Images / Yuri Zvezdny 242–3; Murat Taner 48–9b; thipjang 80–81b; David Tipling 27clb; Luca Trovato 52; Pierre Turtaut 231tl; Universal Images Group / Education Images 211cl; VCG 120–21; VisionsofAmerica / Joe Sohm 142bl; Simon Watson 199br; Whitworth Images 50–51, 125bc; Terrence wijesena 228–9; Wild Africa Nature 137br; wiratgasem 216–17; www.christophe faugere.com 10–11t; xia yuan 113tl; Yagi Studio 81tc; Gary Yeowell 198–9; zhangshuang 190–91.

iStockphoto.com: 4X-image 218bl; Orbon Alija 118t; anzeletti 59cra; bluejayphoto 142–3; Britus 163br; calm_eyes 134–5; DanielHarwardt 204bl; E+ / anzeletti 237bc, / borchee 116–17b, 126–7, / DKart 105, / fotoVoyager 156bl, / mbbirdy 20–21, / miralex 19bc, / PeskyMonkey 88bl, / RelaxFoto.de 23, / stockstudioX 56–7, / svetikd 237bl, / TommL 218–19, / zelg 125bl; Em Campos 238–9; fmajor 171tc; Gatsi 110–11; Infografick 148–9b; KenWiedemann 183bl; kokkai 251; lindsay_imagery 55cr; nicomenijes 59br; OSTILL 165bc; Rat0007 113bl; rchphoto 130fbr; RichardALock 55crb; RomaBlack 4–5; Jonathan Ross 66–7; rusm 10bc; simonbradfield 124–5t, 225fbr; Simonology 226–7; Starcevic

206br; Joerg Steber 130fcr; Onur Yuksel 185br; zorazhuang 112tr.

Map by Free Vector Maps http://freevectormaps.com: 11tc, 12tl, 15ca, 17tl, 18tl, 21tc, 22tl, 24c, 25tl, 26tl, 30tl, 32tl, 35tc, 36tl, 38tl, 41tl, 42tl, 44tl, 47tl, 48tl, 49cr, 52tl, 54tl, 56tl, 57tr, 59tl, 60tl, 62tl, 65tc, 66tl, 68tl, 72tl, 74tl, 77cl, 79tc, 80tl, 82tl, 85cla, 88cra, 89tr, 90tl, 93tc, 94cl, 99tl, 100tl, 101tr, 102tl, 104cla, 107tc, 108tl, 110tl, 112tl, 115tc, 119cla, 120tl, 122tr, 123tr, 124tl, 127tc, 128cla, 130tl, 132tl, 134cla, 136tl, 140tl, 142tr, 143tr, 144tl, 148tl, 150cl, 152tl, 154cla, 157tc, 161cra, 162cla, 163cra, 164tl, 166tl, 169tr, 170cla, 173tl, 174tl, 178ca, 179cr, 181tc, 182tl, 185cla, 186tl, 189ca, 190tl, 192tr, 193tr, 197ca, 199tc, 202cra, 203tr, 205cra, 206tl, 209ca, 211ca, 212ca, 216tl, 219tc, 220tl, 221cr, 223tl, 224tl, 226tl, 229tc, 230tl, 234tl, 236tl, 239tc, 241cla, 242tl, 245cl, 246cla, 248cra, 249tr, 250cla.

Picfair.com: Rui Baiao 130crb; Carlos Sanchez Pereyra 210; Stockimo 156–7; John Such 184.

Robert Harding Picture Library: Neale Clark 128–9t; Frans Lanting 164–5b.

Shutterstock: aodaodaodaod 55cra; Eric Valenne geostory 149cra; Seljan Gurbanova 173crb; Ric Jacyno 129bc; nicolasvoisin44 41crb; Soonthorn Wongsaita 41fbr.

SuperStock: age fotostock / Toño Labra 85cra.

Unsplash: Alexandra Andersson 104crb; Mar Cerdeira 151t; Drew Colins 207; Kylie Docherty 90–91t; Michael Durana 208–9; elCarito / Wild Drawing *Believe in Dreams* 91br; Yuriy Garnaev 72–3; Drew Hays 122–3; Braden Jarvis 212–13; Valentin B. Kremer 187tr; L A L A 132br; Tim Marshall 42crb; Joshua Medway 39br; Random Institute 44–5b; Jailam Rashad 8–9; Hans Reniers 91bc; Heather Shevlin 2; Shounen21 109; Sorasak 6tr; Match Sùmàyà 81tr; Willian Justen de Vasconcellos 131; William Warby 186–7b; Sander Wehkamp 160–61; Fatih Yürür 84.

Cover images:
Front and Back: **Unsplash:** Simon Matzinger.

For further information see: www.dkimages.com